SAUCE

SAUCE

Sonja Lee

Text: Irina Lee   Photographs: Morten Brun

GOLD ST.
PRESS

Contents

Bring flavors together

A good sauce should reinforce the inherent qualities of the main dish's ingredients to create a resonance of flavor. Bear in mind, however, that the role of a sauce is to elevate all the other components of taste on the plate, not to dominate them. In some cases, an overly flavorful sauce will overwhelm a dish. A well-paired sauce can also offer an exciting contrast to the other elements in a dish, creating balance. No matter what role it plays in a dish, a sauce should be pleasing to the eye.

The best-quality ingredients are always the starting point in achieving the best results in a finished sauce. With practice, you'll master the various cooking techniques that can influence the flavor of a sauce. By taste-testing along the way, you can adjust and perfect the flavor and texture of any sauce.

The most effective technique used to make a successful sauce is through the method of reduction. Reduction refers to the evaporation of water through simmering or boiling resulting in concentrated flavor. Every chapter in this book features a different method that may be used to make a sauce. In each chapter I lead you step by step through the process of creating a finished sauce. Every recipe offers at least one suggestion of a dish that the sauce complements. Many of these are classic combinations. You'll also find a cross-referenced list in the back of the book that notes complementary dishes. Of course such a list can never be complete, and you should add your own ideas.

My hope is that this book will inspire you to get going in the kitchen and develop your own sauces. When you have learned the basic techniques, it's easy to create your own unique and delicious variations.

In addition to starting with high-quality ingredients, the best secret I can suggest to becoming a great sauce composer is to exercise a small measure of patience. Everyone knows that practice makes perfect. Don't give up if a sauce is not ideal the first time you make it, because it will get better each time you try it.

I can promise you rewards for your hard work in the kitchen. You can look forward to your dinner guests savoring the very last drop of your fabulous sauce.

Good luck!

Sonja

Jus

A jus is the reduction of natural juices created by the cooking process. The longer you reduce a jus, the more concentrated the flavor.

Lamb jus

This jus complements stuffed tomatoes, glazed vegetables, beans and all lamb dishes, from chops to roast leg of lamb. For this recipe, use leg of lamb, lamb neck, or shank without the bone.

Makes 4 servings:

1½ lb boneless lamb meat
1 whole garlic head
1 onion
3 tablepoons olive oil
1 teaspoon salt
3 tablespoons butter
1–1½ qt (4–6 cups) water

Method:
Cut the meat into ¾-inch cubes. Make the pieces uniform in size so that they will cook evenly. Keeping the garlic skin intact, cut the head in half horizontally. Peel and slice the onion.

Heat the olive oil in a large metal roasting pan over high heat. Add the lamb when the oil begins to smoke slightly. Add the salt and brown the meat well. Be patient and give the meat the time it needs to brown, without turning it too often. (The better the meat is browned, the better the flavor of the jus will be. Do check that it browns evenly and does not burn. This would create an unpleasant bitter taste in the finished jus.)

Maintaining high heat, add the garlic, onion, and 1 tablespoon of the butter and mix well. Let simmer, stirring constantly, until the garlic and onion are golden brown and tender. Watch that the garlic does not burn.

Bring the water to a boil in a separate pot. Once the water has come to a boil, carefully remove the excess fat from the meat and garlic mixture. Tip the roasting pan slightly and slide the meat and garlic to the opposite side. Use a ladle to skim off as much fat as possible. (In French, this process is called *degraisser.* The flavorful residue that remains on the bottom of the pan is called *suc.*)

Add 1 qt of the boiling water. The roasting pan will be so hot that the water will bubble around the meat, dissolving the *suc*. When the liquid has entirely evaporated, add enough water to just cover the surface of the meat. Place a baking sheet over the pan and let it simmer for at least ½ hour. The longer it simmers, the richer the flavor of the finished jus.

Strain the liquid into a saucepan and bring to a boil. Let it simmer uncovered until the liquid is reduced to one-fourth of the original amount, creating a concentrated flavor.

When the liquid has reduced, remove the pan from the heat and add the rest of the butter. Stir carefully with a spoon, not a whisk. (A whisk would add too much air to the jus and give it a pale color.) The jus should not cook after the butter is added, or it may separate.

Continue to stir until the butter is entirely melted and the jus has achieved a smooth thickness. The jus is finished when it has an even, translucent brown color.

1. Heat the olive oil and add the pieces of lamb.

2. Brown the meat well and add the garlic.

3. Add the water.

4. Let it cook for at least ½ hour.

5. Strain and continue to boil the liquid until it is reduced to one-fourth of the original amount.

6. Stir in the butter carefully with a spoon. The jus is ready to serve.

Chicken jus

Chicken jus is the most versatile jus. It is perfect to use with all types of chicken, whether grilled, sautéed, roasted, or poached. Also try the jus in a pasta and vegetable gratin, ravioli, or various types of fish dishes. The jus may even be used as the base for salad vinaigrette. In this recipe, any chicken parts may be used. Use whole chicken parts with as much meat as possible adhering to the bone. It's best to use raw chicken, but cooked can work, too. Use a cleaver or the heel of a large chef's knife to divide the chicken into large, equal-sized pieces before browning.

Makes 4 servings:

1½ lb chicken pieces or 3 whole chicken carcasses
1 whole garlic head
1 onion
3 tablespoons olive oil
1 teaspoon salt
3 tablespoons butter
1–1½ qt (4–6 cups) water

Preparation:
Cut the chicken meat or chicken carcasses into large pieces. Make the pieces uniform in size and thickness so that they will cook evenly.

Keeping the garlic skin intact, cut the head in two horizontally. Peel and slice the onion.

Heat the olive oil in a Dutch oven or roasting pan over high heat. Add the chicken when the oil just begins to smoke. Add the salt and brown the meat well. Be patient and give the meat the time it needs to brown, without turning it too often. (The better the meat is browned, the better the flavor of the jus will be. Do check that it browns evenly and does not burn. This would create an unpleasant bitter taste in the finished jus.)

Maintaining high heat, add the garlic, onion, and 1 tablespoon of the butter and mix well. Let the mixture simmer, stirring constantly, and continue to brown the garlic and onion until they are golden brown and tender. Watch that the garlic does not burn.

Bring the water to a boil in a separate pot. Once the water has come to a boil, carefully remove the excess fat from the meat and onion mixture. Tip the roasting pan slightly and slide the meat and garlic to the opposite side. Use a ladle to skim off almost all of the fat. (In French, this process is called *degraisser.* The flavorful residue that remains on the bottom of the pan is called *suc.*)

Add 1 qt of the boiling water. The roasting pan will be so hot that the water will bubble around the meat, dissolving the *suc.*

When the liquid has entirely evaporated, add enough water to just cover the surface of the meat. Place a baking sheet over the pan and let it simmer for at least ½ hour. The longer it simmers, the richer the flavor of the finished jus.

Strain the liquid into a saucepan and bring to a boil. Let it simmer uncovered until the liquid is reduced to one-fourth of the original amount, creating a concentrated flavor.

When the liquid has reduced, remove from the heat and add the rest of the butter. Stir carefully with a spoon, not a whisk. (A whisk would add too much air to the jus and give it a pale color.) The jus should not cook after the butter is added, or it may separate.

Continue to stir until the butter is entirely melted and the jus has achieved a smooth thickness. The jus is finished when it has an even, translucent brown color.

1. Heat the olive oil and add the chicken pieces.

2. Brown the meat well.

3. Add the onion and garlic.

4. Pour in the water and cook for at least ½ hour.

5. Strain the liquid and continue to boil until it is reduced to one-fourth of the original amount.

6. Stir in the butter carefully with a spoon.
The jus is ready to serve.

Veal jus

Similar to chicken jus, this jus is based on white meat. It is suitable for all the same dishes as chicken jus in addition to all veal dishes. For this jus. use trimmings, including fat, from any cut of veal. It's also possible to use some bones. Make sure there is meat left on the bones. as jus cannot be made out of bones only; both flavor and consistency would suffer.

Makes 4 servings:
1½ lb veal trimmings
1 whole garlic head
1 onion
3 tablespoons olive oil
1 teaspoon salt
3 tablespoons butter
1–1½ quarts (4–6 cups) boiling water

Follow the preparation for Lamb Jus (see recipe page 11).

Pork jus

Pork jus is suitable for all pork dishes, from pork roast and chops to ground pork. For this recipe, use pork neck and/or belly, with bone or without.

Makes 4 servings:
1½ lb pork trimmings
1 whole garlic head
1 onion
3 tablespoons olive oil
1 teaspoon salt
3 tablespoons butter
1–1½ quarts (4–6 cups) boiling water

Follow the preparation for Lamb Jus (see recipe page 11).

Pheasant jus

Pheasant jus goes well with game birds and poultry, such as duck, chicken, or squab, in addition to pheasant. For this recipe, use any whole pheasant parts, with as much meat as possible adhering to the bone. Divide the pheasant into large, equal-sized pieces before browning.

Makes 4 servings:
1½ lb pheasant meat or 5 pheasant carcasses
1 whole garlic head
1 onion
3 tablespoons olive oil
1 teaspoon salt
3 tablespoons butter
1–1½ quarts (4–6 cups) boiling water

Follow the preparation for Lamb Jus (see recipe page 11).

Squab jus

Squab jus goes well with any poultry, especially grouse. For this recipe, use any whole squab parts, with as much meat as possible adhering to the bone.

Makes 4 servings:
1½ lb squab meat or 3 squab carcasses
1 whole garlic head
1 onion
3 tablespoons olive oil
1 teaspoon salt
3 tablespoons butter
1–1½ quarts (4–6 cups) boiling water

Follow the preparation for Lamb Jus (see recipe page 11).

Duck jus

Excellent with poultry, duck jus tastes especially good when paired with chestnuts and grapes. For this recipe, use any whole duck parts, with as much meat as possible adhering to the bone. Divide the duck into large, equal-sized pieces before browning.

Makes 4 servings:
1½ lb duck meat or 3 duck carcasses
1 whole garlic head
1 onion
3 tablespoons olive oil
1 teaspoon salt
3 tablespoons butter
1–1½ quarts (4–6 cups) boiling water

Follow the preparation for Lamb Jus (see recipe page 11).

Beef jus

Beef jus is luxurious and goes well with all beef dishes, pasta, and vegetables. The jus also complements sautéed fish and scallops. Oxtails, tenderloin, and/or beef trimmings that include some fat (for example from ribeye steaks) work well in this recipe.

Makes 4 servings:
1½ lb beef trimmings
1 whole garlic head
5 shallots
3 tablespoons olive oil
1 teaspoon salt
3 tablespoons butter
1–1½ quarts (4–6 cups) boiling water

Follow the preparation for Lamb Jus (see recipe page 11). Peel and slice the shallots and add them at the same time as the garlic.

Rabbit jus

This jus works well with rabbit stew, braised or grilled rabbit, and rabbit rillettes. The jus is also a good accompaniment to grilled vegetables and gnocchi. Rabbit neck, shoulder, leg, and back (saddle) are most suitable for this recipe. Avoid filets because they have no fat.

Makes 4 servings:
1½ lb rabbit meat trimmings
1 whole garlic head
1 onion
5 shallots
3 tablespoons olive oil
1 teaspoon salt
3 tablespoons butter
1–1½ quarts (4–6 cups) boiling water

Follow the preparation for Lamb Jus (see recipe page 11). Peel and slice the shallots and add them at the same time as the garlic.

Lobster jus

This very luxurious jus, made from live lobster, goes well with grilled, steamed, baked, or sautéed lobster. The jus also adds an extra dimension to all kinds of pasta dishes, as well as seafood salad.

Makes 4 servings:
4 live lobsters
1 whole garlic head
1 onion
1 fennel bulb
5 tomatoes
3 tablespoons olive oil
½ teaspoon salt
¼ teaspoon cayenne pepper
1 tablespoon tomato paste

3 tablespoons cognac or whiskey
⅓ cup white wine
⅔ cup water

Bouquet garni:
3 stems fresh basil
3 stems fresh flat-leaf parsley
1 thick slice fresh ginger
1 bay leaf

3 tablespoons butter

Preparation:
Insert a knife into the neck of each lobster and divide the body in two lengthwise. Remove the stomach sac.

Cut the tail into 3 pieces between the joints. Do the same with the claws, cutting between the joints.

Keeping the garlic skin intact, slice the head in half horizontally. Peel the onion and cut in half. Cut each half into small wedges. Cut the fennel in half and then into wedges. Cut each tomato into quarters.

Heat the olive oil in a Dutch oven or large roasting pan over high heat. Add the lobsters when the oil is smoking. Add the salt, and brown the lobster well.

When everything is browned, remove the lobster pieces from the pan. Add the garlic and onion to the pan and let them sizzle for about 5 minutes, until golden and tender. Add the fennel, tomatoes, cayenne pepper, and tomato paste and mix well. Let the mixture sizzle for 5–6 minutes, until the vegetables are tender and the tomatoes have released their juices.

Put the lobster pieces back into the pan, turn up the heat, and stir carefully so that the lobster meat doesn't break up. When everything is smoking hot, pour in the cognac. Light with a match and let it burn without stirring until the flame is extinguished. (The flambéing evaporates the alcohol, so only the flavor remains.)

Pour in the wine and let it simmer until the liquid has reduced by half.

Add the water and bring to a boil. Tie a string around all the herbs to make a bouquet garni. Add the bouquet garni to the pot. (Tying prevents the herbs from floating around and allows you to remove them easily at the end of the cooking process. See page 175 for more information on bouquets garnis.) Cover and let simmer for 45 minutes.

Remove the pan from the heat and take out the bouquet garni. If you like, you can add the butter and serve the dish as a stew. For lobster jus, remove the lobster and strain the liquid through a fine sieve into a clean saucepan. Add the butter and stir it in with a spoon until melted and smooth. (Don't use a whisk because this incorporates too much air into the jus.)

Shellfish jus

If you don't pass this jus through a fine sieve, you can serve it as a soup. Accompany this soup with toast topped with Rouille (See recipe page 42).

Makes 4 servings:
2 live lobsters
5 live crayfish
2 lb white fish trimmings
1 whole garlic head
1 onion
1 fennel bulb
5 tomatoes
3 tablespoons olive oil
½ teaspoon salt
3 tablespoons cognac or whiskey
¼ teaspoon cayenne pepper
1 tablespoon tomato paste
⅓ cup white wine
⅔ cup water

Bouquet garni:
3 stems fresh basil
3 stems fresh flat-leaf parsley
1 thick slice fresh ginger
1 bay leaf

3 tablespoons butter

Preparation:
Insert a knife into the neck of each lobster and divide the body in two lengthwise. Remove the stomach sac.

Cut the tail into 3 pieces between the joints. Do the same with the claws, cutting between the joints.

Insert a knife into the neck of each crayfish and cut the heads in half. Remove the stomach sacs. Cut the tails into big pieces and divide the claws between the joints.

Cut the fish trimmings into big pieces. Keeping the garlic skin intact, slice the head in half horizontally. Peel the onion and cut in half. Cut each half into small wedges. Cut the fennel in half and then into wedges. Cut each tomato into quarters.

Heat the olive oil in a Dutch oven or large roasting pan over high heat. Add the lobster and crayfish when the oil is smoking. Add the salt and brown well.

When everything is browned, pound the mixture with a mallet, so that everything is finely crushed.

Add the cognac. Light with a match and let it burn without stirring until the flame is extinguished. (The flambéing evaporates the alcohol, so that only the flavor remains.)

Add the fish trimmings, garlic, and onion to the pan and let sizzle for about 5 minutes, until everything turns golden and tender. Add the fennel, tomato, and cayenne pepper. Add the tomato paste and mix well. Let the mixture sizzle for 5–6 minutes, until all the vegetables are tender and the tomatoes have released their juices. Pour in the wine and let it simmer until the liquid has reduced by half.

Add the water and bring to a boil. Tie a string around all the herbs to make a bouquet garni. Add the bouquet garni to the pot. (Tying prevents the herbs from floating around and allows you to remove them easily at the end of the cooking process. See page 175 for more information on bouquets garnis.)

Cover the pan and let everything simmer for 45 minutes.

Remove the pan from the heat and take out the bouquet garni. Puree everything with a hand-held mixer. Since there are still pieces of shell in the mixture it may be difficult to process, so alternatively you can use an old-fashioned food mill, grinder, or food processor.

Strain the mixture through a fine sieve into a clean saucepan. Press with the back of a spoon to extract as much liquid as possible, because this is where most of the flavor lies.

Cut the butter into cubes. Stir in one cube at a time with a spoon until melted and smooth. (Don't use a whisk because this incorporates too much air into the jus.)

Veal chop with macaroni gratin

Makes 4 servings:

4 veal chops, 6–7 oz each
2 tablespoons olive oil
2 cups milk
2 cups water
2 whole garlic heads
⅓ lb macaroni
Butter
¾ cup Béchamel (See recipe page 94)
1 cup grated Parmesan
6 tablespoons veal jus (See recipe page 26)

Preparation:
Sauté the chops on both sides in hot olive oil until well browned, and let rest for 10 minutes.

Meanwhile, bring the milk and water to a boil together over high heat with 2 whole garlic heads cut in half horizontally. Add the pasta. Reduce the heat and cook the macaroni lightly for 8 minutes.

Drain the macaroni and remove the garlic. Divide the macaroni into 4 portions. Arrange each portion of macaroni side by side on a buttered baking sheet. Cover each portion with béchamel and sprinkle a generous amount of Parmesan over each.

Bake the macaroni in a preheated oven at 425°F until golden brown.

Heat the veal jus while the macaroni bakes. Serve the pasta piping hot accompanied with the sautéed meat, with veal jus drizzled over.

Mayonnaises

Mayonnaise is an emulsion with oil as its base. The consistency should be thick enough that the sauce is not runny. It's simpler to make a good mayonnaise if all the ingredients are at room temperature before mixing.

Mayonnaise

Mayonnaise is a foundation sauce and the basis for numerous sauces. It's only imagination that limits the use of this sauce for any dish. As for myself, I like mayonnaise for *pommes frites*, eggs, sandwiches, raw vegetables, or cold cooked fish.

Makes 4 servings:

2 egg yolks
1 tablespoon Dijon mustard
½ teaspoon salt
½ teaspoon cayenne pepper
⅔ cup grapeseed oil
1 teaspoon white wine vinegar

Preparation:
Place the egg yolks in a bowl together with the mustard, salt, and cayenne pepper. Whisk well.

Add the oil in a thin stream while whisking constantly.

When three-quarters of the oil has been added and the mayonnaise begins to thicken, add the vinegar in a thin stream while continuing to whisking. The vinegar will make the consistency of the mayonnaise thinner.

Add the rest of the oil, little by little, so the mayonnaise thickens again. (In French, this is called *monter*—to mount—the mayonnaise.) Continue to whisk the mayonnaise until it reaches a thick, spreadable consistency.

1. Place the egg yolks in a bowl together with the mustard, salt, and cayenne pepper. Add most of the oil in a thin stream while whisking. Add the vinegar along the way.

2. The mayonnaise is ready to serve.

Aioli

Aioli is a thick mayonnaise-based sauce originally from Provence. The name comes from *ai*, which means garlic, and *oli*, which means oil. Aioli is often served with hard-boiled eggs, salads, snails, and cold meat and fish dishes. It can also be served as a dip for vegetables.

Makes 4 servings:
1 whole garlic head
2 egg yolks
1 tablespoon Dijon mustard
½ teaspoon salt
½ teaspoon ground white pepper
⅓ cup grapeseed oil
1 teaspoon white wine vinegar

Preparation:
Preheat the oven to 400°F. Divide the garlic into cloves, leaving skins on, and spread on a baking sheet. Bake the cloves for about 20 minutes, until tender.

Squeeze the garlic pulp from the skins and place in a bowl. Add the egg yolks together with the mustard, salt, and pepper. Whisk well.

Add the oil in a thin stream while whisking constantly.

When three-quarters of the oil has been added and the aioli begins to thicken, add the vinegar in a thin stream while continuing to whisk. The vinegar will make the consistency of the aioli thinner.

Add the rest of the oil, little by little, so the aioli thickens again. Continue to whisk the consistency is correct.

Cocktail sauce

This mayonnaise-based cocktail sauce (similar to thousand-island dressing) makes an ideal accompaniment to avocado as well as crab, shrimp, and all other types of shellfish. It also serves well as a salad dressing. In France it is common to use a little cognac in this sauce as a flavor booster.

Makes 4 servings:
1 egg yolk
½ teaspoon salt
½ teaspoon cayenne pepper
1 tablespoon mustard
1 tablespoon white vinegar
6 tablespoons grapeseed oil
1 tablespoon cognac
2 tablespoons ketchup
½ teaspoon Worcestershire sauce

Preparation:
Whisk the egg yolk, salt, cayenne pepper, mustard, and vinegar in a bowl. Add the oil in a thin stream while constantly whisking. Continue to whisk until the consistency is very thick.

Add the cognac, ketchup, and Worcestershire sauce, and mix well. This will give the sauce a slightly thinner consistency.

Rémoulade

Rémoulade is a wonderful accompaniment to floured or breaded meat and fish. It's also served with roast beef and other thinly sliced meats.

Makes 4 servings:
¾ cup Mayonnaise (See recipe page 37)
1 teaspoon white vinegar
1 tablespoon finely chopped gherkins
1 tablespoon finely chopped capers
1 tablespoon finely chopped tarragon
1 tablespoon finely chopped chives
½ crushed garlic clove
½ teaspoon sugar

Preparation:
Mix the mayonnaise with all of the other ingredients. The rémoulade is ready to serve.

Tartar sauce

This is perfect for deep-fried fish and shellfish, cold grilled meat, and raw or cooked chilled vegetables.

Makes 4 servings:
¾ cup Mayonnaise (See recipe page 37)
3 tablespoons finely chopped gherkins
3 tablespoons finely chopped capers
3 tablespoons finely chopped flat-leaf parsley
1 tablespoon finely chopped onion
½ teaspoon Tabasco

Preparation:
Mix the mayonnaise with all of the other ingredients. The tartar sauce is ready to serve.

Garlic mayonnaise

Garlic mayonnaise is a good accompaniment to raw vegetables or a complement to salads.

Makes 4 servings:
4 anchovy filets
2 crushed garlic cloves
2 tablespoons finely chopped chive
¾ cup Mayonnaise (See recipe page 37)

Preparation:
Smash the anchovies into a paste with a fork. Mix the anchovy paste with the garlic and chives, and add the mayonnaise. Fold all the ingredients together.

Rouille

Rouille is traditionally served on toast alongside a fish or shellfish soup. The toast with rouille can be placed on the soup or served on the side. In many places in France, the rouille toast is topped with grated Gruyère.

Makes 4 servings:
1 large potato
2 crushed garlic cloves
1 teaspoon Tabasco
½ teaspoon cayenne pepper
½ teaspoon saffron
¼ cup ketchup
½ teaspoon salt
1 egg yolk
6 tablespoons olive oil

Preparation:
Peel and boil the potato. Drain the potato and set aside until the moisture evaporates. While the potato is still warm, mash it with a fork. Add the garlic, Tabasco, cayenne pepper, saffron, ketchup, and salt. Add the egg yolk and mix well.

Pour in the olive oil in a thin stream, whisking constantly, until the mixture has a thick and even consistency.

Caesar dressing

This is the classic Caesar dressing, which is served with romaine lettuce. The lettuce is topped with croutons, Parmesan, and anchovy filets. The dressing is also suitable for various other types of salads, depending on your own taste.

Makes 4 servings:
6 anchovy filets
2 egg yolks
2 tablespoons Dijon mustard
3 tablespoons grapeseed oil
3 tablespoons olive oil
2 teaspoons Worcestershire sauce
3 tablespoons fresh lemon juice
2 crushed garlic cloves
½ teaspoon salt
½ teaspoon pepper

Preparation:
Place the anchovy filets, egg yolks, and mustard in a blender and puree until the mixture has an even consistency. Add the grapeseed and olive oils in a thin stream, whisking constantly, until the dressing has a thick and even consistency.

Blend in the Worcestershire sauce, lemon juice, and garlic. Add salt and pepper to taste.

Parmesan mayonnaise

Try this with cold chicken or as a salad dressing.

Makes 4 servings:
¾ cup Mayonnaise (See recipe page 37)
1 cup grated Parmesan
2 crushed garlic cloves
2 tablespoons sherry vinegar
3 tablespoons water
½ teaspoon cayenne pepper

Preparation:
Mix the mayonnaise with all of the other ingredients. The Parmesan mayonnaise is ready to serve.

Chicken salad with parmesan mayonnaise

Makes 4 servings:

1 lb mixed salad greens, such as frisée, arugula, and red leaf lettuce
1 roasted chicken
¾ cup Parmesan mayonnaise (See recipe page 43)
Freshly grated Parmesan
Flat-leaf parsley leaves
Snipped fresh chives

Preparation:
Carefully wash and dry the salad greens, tear them into pieces, and place them in a salad bowl.

If the chicken is still warm, remove the skin and tear the meat into strips. If the chicken is cold, cut it into serving pieces.

Arrange the chicken on top of the salad and pour on the Parmesan mayonnaise. Toss the salad gently.

Top with the freshly grated Parmesan and the herbs, and serve.

Oil-based sauces

Oil-based sauces are made without heat. It's essential to use the best raw materials for the best flavor in the finished dish.

Basil vinaigrette

Basil vinaigrette tastes incredibly good with a simple mixture of tomatoes and mozzarella.

Makes 4 servings:

1 clove garlic
2 tablespoons finely chopped basil
1 tablespoon mustard
1 tablespoon honey
3 tablespoons sherry vinegar
1 cup olive oil
½ teaspoon salt
½ teaspoon pepper

Preparation:
Peel the garlic and crush together with the basil with a mortar and pestle.

Transfer to a bowl and stir in the mustard, honey, and vinegar.

Add the olive oil in a thin stream, whisking constantly. Add salt and pepper. The vinaigrette is ready to serve.

1. Place the garlic and basil in the mortar.

2. Crush together well.

3. Add the mustard, honey, vinegar, salt, and pepper.

4. Mix well.

5. Whisk in the olive oil.

6. The vinaigrette is ready to serve.

Mustard vinaigrette

Mustard vinaigrette is an excellent accompaniment to cucumber salad, grated carrot salad, and other raw vegetable salads.

Makes 4 servings:

1 tablespoon Dijon mustard
1 teaspoon dry mustard
1 egg yolk
½ teaspoon salt
½ teaspoon pepper
1 tablespoon white wine vinegar
½ cup grapeseed oil

Preparation:
Mix the mustards, egg yolk, salt, pepper, and vinegar with a fork. Add the oil slowly in a thin stream, stirring constantly. Continue whisking until the vinaigrette thickens to a full-bodied consistency.

1. Mix the mustard, egg yolk, salt, pepper, and vinegar.
Whisk in the oil, and the vinaigrette is ready to serve.

Ravigotte sauce

Ravigotte sauce is an excellent accompaniment to crayfish, fish, and cold meat dishes.

Makes 4 servings:
3 tablespoons white wine vinegar
1 tablespoon Dijon mustard
½ teaspoon salt
½ teaspoon ground white pepper
2 tablespoons finely chopped white onion
2 teaspoons finely chopped small capers
1 tablespoon chopped flat-leaf parsley
1 tablespoon chopped fresh chives
½ cup grapeseed oil

Preparation:
Mix the vinegar, mustard, salt, and pepper in a bowl. Add the onion, capers, and herbs and mix well.

Add the oil slowly in a thin stream, whisking constantly. Continue whisking until the vinaigrette thickens.

Lemon vinaigrette

Lemon vinaigrette is a fine accompaniment for fish, crayfish, vegetables, and salads.

Makes 4 servings:
Juice of 3 lemons
Grated zest of 1 lemon
¼ teaspoon salt
¼ teaspoon ground white pepper
⅛ teaspoon sugar
½ cup olive oil

Preparation:
Mix the lemon juice, zest, salt, and pepper, and sugar with a whisk. Add the oil slowly in a thin stream, whisking constantly. Continue whisking until the vinaigrette thickens.

The lemon vinaigrette will keep, refrigerated, for 2 days. Mix well before serving.

Chile vinaigrette

Chile vinaigrette is very good with shellfish salads, especially grilled octopus and arugula.

Makes 4 servings:
2 red chiles, finely chopped
2 green chiles, finely chopped
1 crushed clove garlic
1 tablespoon finely chopped flat-leaf parsley
1 tablespoon finely chopped shallot
1 teaspoon sugar
1 teaspoon dry mustard
1 tablespoon sherry vinegar
½ cup grapeseed oil

Preparation:
Mix the red and green chiles, garlic, parsley, shallot, sugar, mustard, and vinegar with a fork. Add the oil slowly in a thin stream, whisking constantly. Continue whisking until the vinaigrette thickens.

Honey vinaigrette

Honey vinaigrette is an excellent accompaniment to frisée salad and other bitter greens salads. The sweet honey balances their bite. Try this with French chèvre.

Makes 4 servings:
1 tablespoon whole-grain mustard
1 teaspoon dry mustard
1 tablespoon honey
1 teaspoon salt
1 teaspoon ground black pepper
1 tablespoon sherry vinegar
½ cup vegetable oil

Preparation:
Mix the mustards, honey, salt, pepper, and vinegar with a fork. Add the oil slowly in a thin stream, whisking constantly. Continue whisking until the vinaigrette thickens.

Flat-leaf parsley vinaigrette

Flat-leaf parsley vinaigrette tastes wonderful with many egg dishes and can also be used as a dressing for various salads.

Makes 4 servings:
1 teaspoon Dijon mustard
3 tablespoons finely chopped flat-leaf parsley
½ teaspoon sugar
1 crushed garlic clove
1 egg yolk
1 tablespoon balsamic vinegar
½ cup grapeseed oil

Preparation:
Mix the mustard, parsley, sugar, garlic, egg yolk, and vinegar with a fork. Add the oil slowly in a thin stream, whisking constantly. Continue whisking until the sauce thickens.

Shallot vinaigrette

Shallot vinaigrette can top raw oysters or dress shellfish salads. It is also good with mâche salads.

Makes 4 servings:
4 shallots, finely chopped
1 tablespoon finely chopped flat-leaf parsley
½ teaspoon salt
½ teaspoon pepper
2 tablespoons sherry vinegar
½ cup olive oil

Preparation:
Mix shallots, parsley, salt, pepper, and vinegar with a fork. Add the oil slowly in a thin stream, whisking constantly. Continue whisking until the vinaigrette thickens.

Tapenade vinaigrette

Try tapenade vinaigrette with a warm chèvre salad or warm vegetable bruschetta. It's also wonderful with a raw fennel salad.

Makes 4 servings:
2 tablespoons tapenade
1 teaspoon Dijon mustard
1 crushed garlic clove
½ teaspoon salt
½ teaspoon pepper
1 tablespoon sherry vinegar
½ cup olive oil

Preparation:
Mix tapenade, mustard, garlic, salt, pepper, and vinegar with a fork. Add the oil slowly in a thin stream, whisking constantly. Continue whisking until the vinaigrette thickens.

Balsamic vinaigrette

This simple, classic vinaigrette is suitable for most green salads.

Makes 4 servings:
1 tablespoon Dijon mustard
1 teaspoon salt
½ teaspoon pepper
1 teaspoon sugar
3 tablespoons balsamic vinegar
½ cup olive oil

Preparation:
Mix mustard, salt, pepper, sugar, and vinegar with a fork. Add the oil slowly in a thin stream, whisking constantly. Continue whisking until the vinaigrette thickens.

Anchoïade

Anchoïade is a traditional sauce from Provence and the south of France. The sauce is served as a dip for raw or cold cooked vegetables and cold cooked fish.

Makes 4 servings:
3 cloves garlic
6 stems of flat-leaf parsley
10 salt-packed anchovy filets
1 teaspoon sherry vinegar
6 tablespoons olive oil

Preparation:
Peel the garlic cloves and slice them in half lengthwise. Remove any little green sprout in the center. Crush the garlic in a mortar or with a fork in a bowl until it has the consistency of a coarse puree.

Wash the parsley, pluck off all the leaves, and finely chop them. Set aside.

Rinse the anchovies well with water to remove excess salt. Crush the anchovies together with the garlic until the mixture has a smooth consistency. Stir in the sherry vinegar.

Add the olive oil slowly in a thin stream, whisking constantly. Continue whisking vigorously until the vinaigrette thickens.

Add the chopped parsley. The anchoïade is ready to serve.

Cambridge sauce

This traditional English sauce is ideal for cold meat, fish, or raw vegetables.

Makes 4 servings:
4 anchovy filets
3 hard-boiled egg yolks
1 tablespoon small capers
1 tablespoon dry mustard
1 tablespoon red wine vinegar
2 tablespoons chopped fresh tarragon
1 tablespoon chopped fresh chervil
1 tablespoon chopped flat-leaf parsley
1 tablespoon chopped fresh chives
6 tablespoons grapeseed oil

Preparation:
Mash the anchovy filets in a mortar or a bowl. Add the egg yolks and capers and mash these into the mixture. Add the mustard, vinegar, and all the chopped herbs. Mix well.

Add the oil slowly in a thin stream, whisking constantly. Continue whisking until the vinaigrette thickens.

Eggplant salad with balsamic vinaigrette

Makes 4 servings:

8 globe eggplants
12 sprigs thyme
1 teaspoon salt
½ teaspoon ground white pepper
1 whole head garlic
6 tablespoons olive oil
Juice of ½ lemon
4 oz mesclun or arugula
12–24 slices Tomato Confit (See recipe page 177)
6 tablespoons Balsamic Vinaigrette (See recipe page 63)
Balsamic vinegar
Fresh chèvre (optional)
Olive-oil rubbed toasts (optional)

Preparation:
Preheat the oven to 350°F. Cut 6 of the eggplants in half lengthwise. Cut crosshatch patterns on the inside of each half, scoring halfway down through the flesh towards the skin. Arrange the eggplants cut side up on a baking sheet. Lay a thyme sprig on top of each eggplant. Sprinkle salt and pepper over all. Cut the garlic head in half horizontally and remove the cloves from one side. Place them on and around the eggplant. Place the intact half a garlic head cut side up on the pan as well. Drizzle the olive oil over all. Bake for 35 minutes. If the eggplant begins to turn brown, cover the pan with aluminum foil.

When the eggplant is ready, scoop out the flesh with a spoon and place in a pan. Set on low heat.

Let the eggplant flesh simmer for 1 hour, stirring frequently. (Simmering reduces eggplant's high moisture content and concentrates its flavor.) When the puree is almost completely dry, add the salt, pepper, and lemon juice. Remove the rest of the garlic from the head, except for 1 clove, and squeeze the garlic pulp into the puree. Set the pan aside. Transfer the puree to a bowl and let it cool.

While the eggplant is simmering, halve the remaining 2 eggplants lengthwise and cut lengthwise into ¼-inch-thick slices. Rub the slices with salt, pepper, olive oil, and the remaining garlic clove. Sauté the slices in a pan with olive oil until they are browned on both sides. Alternatively, the eggplant slices may be grilled.

Arrange arugula on each plate for serving. Divide the eggplant puree and sautéed slices among the plates, placing them on each bed of arugula. Top each salad with tomato confit.

Drizzle the balsamic vinaigrette over the top of each salad, and sprinkle with balsamic vinegar as well. Top with chèvre and accompany with toasts, if desired.

Eggplant salad with balsamic vinaigrette

Cream-based sauces

These sauces simmer for a long while to concentrate their flavors. A good splash of heavy cream ensures a well-rounded flavor and smooth texture.

Mushroom cream

I often use this cream sauce for pasta. Mushroom cream complements all types of white meat, such as pork or chicken, very nicely.

Makes 4 servings:

1 tablespoon olive oil
2 cups sliced mushrooms
1 clove garlic
3 finely chopped shallots
1 tablespoon butter
3 tablespoons Chicken Stock (See recipe page 170)
½ cup heavy cream
3 tablespoons crème fraîche
½ teaspoon salt
½ teaspoon pepper

Preparation:
Heat the olive oil in a sauté pan over medium-high heat. Add the mushrooms and brown them well. Crush the garlic and place it in the pan with the shallots and butter. Let the mixture cook together until the shallots become tender and golden brown.

Add the chicken stock and let it simmer until the liquid has evaporated.

Add the heavy cream and crème fraîche and let simmer until the liquid is reduced by half. Serve as is, or blend with a hand-held mixer to a smooth consistency. Add salt and pepper before serving.

1. Brown the mushrooms. Add shallots, garlic, and butter.

2. Add the chicken stock.

3. Add cream and crème fraîche.

4. Let the mixture simmer until the mushroom cream is ready to serve.

Roquefort cream

This sauce is a great accompaniment to all types of grilled meat. Serve with entrecôte (ribeye steak) to re-create a French bistro classic at home.

Makes 4 servings:
6 oz Roquefort
½ cup crème fraîche
6 tablespoons Demi-glace (See recipe page 171)

Preparation:
Melt the Roquefort in a pan over medium heat. Add the crème fraîche and mix well until everything has melted. Add the demi-glace. Let it simmer for 2–3 minutes to thicken into a sauce, and serve.

Mustard cream

Mustard cream goes well with all grilled meat, especially pork and chicken.

Makes 4 servings:
½ cup crème fraîche
¼ cup Dijon mustard
6 tablespoons Demi-glace (See recipe page 171)

Preparation:
Melt the crème fraîche in a saucepan over medium heat and add the mustard. Add the demi-glace and let it simmer for 2–3 minutes, stirring constantly. Strain the sauce through a sieve, and serve.

Morel cream

Prized morel mushrooms pop up in the spring after the frost has departed, then flourish with the warmer weather that arrives in April. Morel cream is traditionally served with asparagus, but also tastes very good with veal or fish. Other mushrooms may be substituted for the morels.

Makes 4 servings:
1 tablespoon butter
3 shallots, finely chopped
6 oz fresh morels
3 tablespoons Chicken Stock (See recipe page 170)
½ cup heavy cream
3 tablespoons crème fraîche
½ teaspoon salt
½ teaspoon pepper

Preparation:
Melt the butter in a pan over medium-high heat and add the shallots. Sauté until the shallots become tender and golden brown.

Clean and dry the morels well and cut them into small pieces. Add the morels to the pan and let them cook with the shallots until they are tender.

Add the chicken stock and let it simmer until the liquid has reduced by half.

Finally, add the cream and crème fraîche and let simmer until reduced by half. Blend with a hand-held mixer until smooth. Add salt and pepper, and serve.

Herb cream

Try this herb cream the next time you serve lamb. It's a simple way to make a full-flavored sauce.

Makes 4 servings:
1 cup heavy cream
3 tablespoons crème fraîche
1 teaspoon finely chopped rosemary
1 teaspoon finely chopped thyme
2 cloves crushed garlic
1 tablespoon whole-grain mustard
2 tablespoons finely chopped
flat-leaf parsley
2 tablespoons finely chopped chives
½ teaspoon salt
½ teaspoon pepper

Preparation:
Combine the cream and crème fraîche in a saucepan together with the rosemary, thyme, and garlic. Cook over low heat for 15 minutes.

Strain the sauce through a sieve. Stir in the mustard, remaining herbs, salt, and pepper, and serve.

Fish velouté

This sauce complements fish casseroles, steamed fish, and vegetables.

Makes 4 servings:
2 cups Mussel Stock (See recipe page 159)
2 tablespoons butter
¼ cup flour
1 tablespoon minced flat-leaf parsley
1 tablespoon finely chopped chives
½ teaspoon salt
½ teaspoon pepper

Preparation:
Warm up the mussel stock in a saucepan.

Melt the butter in another saucepan over medium heat. Add the flour and stir well. Ladle in the mussel stock little by little, while constantly stirring. Let the sauce simmer, stirring, for 10 minutes.

Strain the sauce through a sieve if clumps form. Stir in the fresh herbs, salt, and pepper, and serve.

Horseradish cream

This sharp-flavored sauce tastes particularly good with cold meat and fish dishes or raw vegetables. It's also nice on a baked potato, with a bit of crisp fried bacon.

Makes 4 servings:
2 slices white bread, crusts trimmed
¼ cup milk
1 cup grated fresh horseradish
½ teaspoon salt
½ teaspoon sugar
1 teaspoon white wine vinegar
1¼ cups crème fraîche

Preparation:
Lay the bread slices in a bowl and cover with the milk. Add the horseradish, salt, sugar, and vinegar and mix everything to a smooth consistency. Fold in the crème fraîche, and serve.

Butter-based sauces

Many of the best-known dishes of the classic French table feature luxurious sauces based on sweet, creamy butter.

Béarnaise

Béarnaise is among the basic sauces of the French kitchen. It includes eggs and resembles hollandaise. The classic way to serve béarnaise is with a hearty steak and *pommes frites*. The sauce can be used as a dip for vegetables, or can be served with grilled meat and fish dishes.

Makes 4 servings:

½ cup butter
3 small shallots
2 tablespoons finely chopped tarragon
2 tablespoons finely chopped chervil
6 tablespoons white wine vinegar
6 tablespoons white wine
½ tablespoon whole white peppercorns
4 egg yolks
2 tablespoons water
½ teaspoon salt
¼ teaspoon cayenne pepper

Preparation:
The first step in this sauce is to clarify the butter, which means to separate the milk solids from the pure fat.

Gently melt the butter in a warm saucepan. As it melts, a milky white portion will sink to the bottom of the pan, leaving a layer of clear yellow liquid butter. This clear yellow liquid is the clarified butter. When the butter has separated, take a ladle and carefully remove the clear clarified butter. Discard the milky substance. Set aside the clarified butter.

Peel and finely chop the shallots. Place the shallots in a saucepan together with half of the tarragon and chervil, the vinegar, and the white wine. Crush the pepper in a mortar and add it to the pan. Heat the ingredients over low heat and let simmer for 5–10 minutes, until all the liquid has evaporated. (This is called a reduction.)

Add the egg yolks to the reduction and whisk vigorously to create an airy consistency. Add most of the clarified butter in a thin stream, whisking constantly. This will give the sauce a thick and full-bodied consistency. Whip in the 2 tablespoons water so that the sauce becomes thinner and lighter in color. Whip in the remaining clarified butter and season with salt and cayenne pepper.

Add the rest of the herbs and serve the sauce at once. Alternatively, strain the sauce through a sieve before adding the rest of the herbs.

After the sauce is finished, it must not be warmed up again. This would cause it to "break," or separate into fat and liquid. The sauce can stay warm in a warm-water bath, covered with a lid or plastic wrap. This will prevent a skin from forming on the top.

1. Mix the tarragon, chervil, white wine vinegar,
white wine, and white pepper.

2. Let it simmer until the liquid has evaporated.

3. Add the egg yolks.

4. Whisk vigorously.

5. Add the butter in a thin stream
while whisking constantly.

6. Strain the sauce through a sieve, if desired.

7. Add the rest of the herbs, and the sauce is ready to serve.

Beurre blanc

Beurre blanc is a classic French butter-based sauce that especially complements hot fish and shellfish dishes. The sauce can be used as a base for numerous variations. Add chopped tomatoes at the end to make *beurre tomat*. Adding flat-leaf parsley makes it into *beurre persillé*.

Makes 4 servings:

4 shallots
6 tablespoons white wine
3 tablespoons white wine vinegar
½ teaspoon whole black peppercorns
¾ cup cold butter
½ teaspoon salt
½ teaspoon cayenne pepper

Preparation:
Peel and finely chop the shallots and place them in a saucepan. Add the white wine, vinegar, and peppercorns. Simmer over medium heat until one-quarter of the liquid remains.

Chop the cold butter into ½-inch cubes. Remove the pan from the heat and whisk in the butter cube by cube, until the consistency thickens. (In French, this process is called *monter,* or "to mount".) If the sauce is heated again, it will break, or separate.

Season with salt and cayenne pepper. Strain the sauce through a sieve, pressing with the back of a spoon to extract as much liquid as possible, and serve.

1. Combine finely chopped shallots, white wine, vinegar, and pepper in a pan.

2. Reduce the liquid to one-quarter of the original amount.

3. Whisk in the butter cubes.

4. Strain the sauce.

5. Press the sauce through the sieve with a spoon.

6. Season with salt and cayenne pepper.
The sauce is ready to serve.

Béchamel

Béchamel is the most classic of all white sauces. It's well suited to any type of gratin, such as vegetable and pasta gratin.

Makes 4 servings:
2 tablespoons butter
¼ cup flour
2 cups milk
½ teaspoon salt
½ teaspoon white pepper
¼ teaspoon grated nutmeg

Preparation:
Melt the butter in a heavy-bottomed pan, preferably cast iron, over low heat. Add the flour and stir together with a whisk to cook lightly without browning. Add the milk while whisking vigorously so that the mixture won't get lumpy. Add salt, pepper, and grated nutmeg to taste.

Let the béchamel cook for at least 10 minutes, stirring constantly. Pour the sauce through a fine sieve to remove potential lumps. The béchamel is now ready to serve.

Mornay sauce

Mornay sauce is based on béchamel. It's served with many classic French egg dishes, such as eggs Florentine. The sauce is also ideal for gratin of vegetables, particularly cauliflower.

Makes 4 servings:
Béchamel (See recipe at left)
1 egg yolk
3 tablespoons grated Gruyère
½ tablespoon butter

Preparation:
Put the béchamel sauce in a warm-water bath. Fill a large pan with an inch of water and place it over low heat. Place a smaller saucepan holding the sauce in this warm-water bath. Do not let the water temperature exceed 175°F. The sauce should just keep warm and not boil.

Add the egg yolk and the cheese and whisk well. To prevent a skin from forming, carefully smear a lump of butter over the surface. Keep the sauce warm in the warm-water bath until it is served.

Mousseline

This sauce is excellent with cooked asparagus.

Makes 4 servings:
2 egg yolks
½ cup melted butter
½ teaspoon salt
¼ teaspoon cayenne pepper
Juice of ½ lemon
1 cup heavy cream

Preparation:
This sauce should be made in a warm-water bath. Fill a large pan with an inch of water and place it over low heat. Place a smaller saucepan in the warm-water bath.

Add the egg yolks and whisk until they are airy and almost white. Carefully pour the melted butter into the eggs, whisking constantly. Add the salt, cayenne pepper, and lemon juice. Continue to whisk. Do not let the water temperature exceed 175°F. The sauce should just keep warm and not boil.

Pour the sauce through a fine sieve into a stainless-steel bowl to remove lumps. Place the bowl in the warm-water bath or pour the strained mixture back into the pan and return it to the warm-water bath.

Whip the cream until stiff and fold it carefully into the mixture. The sauce is ready to serve.

Hollandaise

Hollandaise is an egg-based sauce that is whipped up with butter. Personally, I think the best way to serve hollandaise is with cooked green asparagus, topped with a few drops of lemon juice. It can also be used for gratins and desserts. If served with desserts, replace the salt with sugar and eliminate the pepper.

Makes 4 servings:
⅔ cup butter
2 egg yolks
Juice of ¼ lemon
½ teaspoon salt
½ teaspoon ground white pepper

Preparation:
Melt the butter in a saucepan over low heat. Place the egg yolks in a separate pan and set over low heat. Whisk the egg yolks by hand until they are airy and almost white, and barely lukewarm. Regulate the heat by moving the pan back and forth over the heat.

Remove the pan from the heat and whisk vigorously and slowly and carefully pour the melted butter into the eggs. Add the lemon juice, salt, and white pepper. The hollandaise is ready to serve.

Beurre maître d'hôtel

Beurre maître d'hôtel is a classic herb butter served with grilled meat and fish dishes. In the classical French kitchen, the flavored butter is shaped into disks for serving. Wrap the butter in plastic and shape it into a log, then put it into the refrigerator to chill before slicing. Alternatively, the butter may be placed in a pastry bag and applied decoratively, or simply served from the bowl with a spoon.

Makes 4 servings:
⅓ cup butter
5 stems flat-leaf parsley
Juice of ½ lemon
½ teaspoon cayenne pepper
½ teaspoon salt

Preparation:
Take the butter out of the refrigerator a good while before it will be used and let it come to room temperature.

Wash and dry the parsley. Pluck and finely chop the leaves. Put the butter in a small bowl and add the parsley, lemon juice, cayenne pepper, and salt. Mix well. The butter is ready to serve.

Herb butter

This herb butter is suitable for all types of grilled meat, fish, or vegetable dishes. Melting the herb butter over a pot-au-feu adds a special twist to the French classic.

Makes 4 servings:
⅓ cup butter
5 stems flat-leaf parsley
2 cloves garlic
Juice of ½ lemon
½ teaspoon cayenne pepper
½ teaspoon salt

Preparation:
Take the butter out of the refrigerator a good while before it will be used and let it come to room temperature.

Wash and dry the parsley. Pluck and finely chop the leaves. Peel the garlic and crush it in a mortar. Put the butter in a small bowl and add the parsley, garlic, lemon juice, cayenne pepper, and salt. Mix well. The butter is ready to serve.

Grenobloise butter

This butter is served with fried fish and is especially good with those in the flounder family.

Makes 4 servings:
2 slices white country bread, crusts removed
⅓ cup butter
2 tablespoons olive oil
1 lemon
2 tablespoons large capers

Preparation:
Cut the bread into cubes. Put half the butter and half the olive oil in a frying pan over medium-high heat and sauté the bread cubes into crispy croutons. Transfer the croutons to a plate lined with paper towels to drain the excess fat. Set aside.

Peel the lemon and cut out sections by inserting the knife between the flesh and membrane of each section.

Warm the remaining olive oil in a pan over medium-high heat and add the capers. Let them sizzle until they are lightly browned. Add the remaining butter and let brown. Add the lemon sections when the butter is brown.

Sprinkle the croutons over the fish and pour the Grenobloise butter over the top. Serve.

Beurre meunière

Beurre meunière is served with all types of fish dishes.

Makes 4 servings:
3 tablespoons butter
Juice of 1 lemon

Preparation:
Melt the butter in a saucepan over low heat until it starts to foam. Brown the butter lightly. This goes quite fast, so be careful that the butter doesn't burn. As soon as the butter is nut-brown, remove the pan from the heat. Add the lemon juice, and the butter is ready to serve.

Anchovy butter

If you are serving fried fish, this butter is an excellent accompaniment. It is also delicious served with a piece of toast.

Makes 4 servings:
8 anchovy filets
3 tablespoons butter, at room temperature
1 tablespoon chopped flat-leaf parsley
¼ teaspoon cayenne pepper
½ teaspoon salt

Preparation:
Mash the anchovies well, then mix with the rest of the ingredients. Refrigerate until ready to serve.

Garlic butter

Garlic butter is all-purpose and is ideal with cooked, fried, and baked potatoes or with grilled meat and fish.

Makes 4 servings:
3 tablespoons butter, at room temperature
4 cloves garlic, finely chopped
2 tablespoons finely chopped chives
¼ teaspoon cayenne pepper
½ teaspoon salt

Preparation:
Mix all the ingredients together. Refrigerate until ready to serve.

Beurre noisette

Beurre noisette is served with fried fish, and probably is best as an accompaniment to poached skate. It seems simple to make this sauce, but be careful that the butter doesn't burn.

Makes 4 servings:
⅔ cup butter

Preparation:
Melt ½ cup of the butter over medium to medium-low heat and let it brown well, being careful not to let it burn.

Cut the rest of the butter into cubes.

When the butter begins to brown, remove the pan from the heat and add the butter cubes one at a time and stir with a spoon. This will thicken the butter a little. The *beurre noisette* is ready to serve.

Choron sauce

Serve Choron sauce with warm grilled meat and fish dishes.

Makes 4 servings:
¾ cup Béarnaise (See recipe page 81)
3 tablespoons Tomato Sauce (See recipe page 120)

Preparation:
Mix the 2 sauces well, and the Choron sauce is ready to serve.

Sauce albert

This sauce is perfect for fish and shellfish dishes.

Makes 4 servings:
6 tablespoons Chicken Stock (See recipe page 170)
2 tablespoons finely grated horseradish
6 tablespoons Beurre Blanc (See recipe page 89)
1 egg yolk
1 tablespoon dry mustard
1 tablespoon sherry vinegar

Preparation:
Put the chicken stock and horseradish in a pan over medium heat and simmer for 3 minutes. Add the beurre blanc and let simmer until half the liquid has evaporated.

Strain the mixture into a new pan and bring to a boil over medium heat. Remove the pan from the heat and whisk in the egg yolk.

Just before serving, mix the mustard and vinegar in a clean bowl and pour this mixture into the pan, stirring well. Do not reheat the sauce after the mustard-vinegar mixture is added, or it will coagulate and be ruined.

Asparagus with hollandaise

Makes 4 servings:

25–30 asparagus spears
3 tablespoons olive oil
1 teaspoon salt
¾ cup Chicken Stock or Vegetable Stock
(See recipe page 170 or 167)
¾ cup Hollandaise (See recipe page 95)
Flat-leaf parsley leaves

Preparation:
Peel the asparagus and trim away the woody bottoms.

Heat 3 tablespoons of the olive oil in a sauté pan. Place the asparagus in the pan and sprinkle with the salt. Roll the asparagus in the hot oil for 4 minutes, until it glistens.

Add the stock and simmer for 3–4 minutes. Insert a knife into the asparagus to see if it is ready. This dish is best when the asparagus is served al dente.

Serve the asparagus with a generous amount of hollandaise. This dish may be served either warm or cold.

Fruit and vegetable sauces

These sauces reveal the best of the raw ingredients that compose them. Many have a lovely vibrant color, which adds beauty as well as flavor to the finished dish.

Pesto

Pesto is an herb-based sauce drawing its character from basil. In this classic recipe for pesto, use aged pecorino. If pecorino is not available, use Parmesan. Pesto is best served with pasta, salads, or fish. Try topping your favorite pizza with pesto.

Makes 4 servings:

2 cups fresh basil leaves
2 cloves garlic
¼ cup pine nuts
¼ cup grated aged pecorino
6 tablespoons olive oil

Preparation:
Heat a dry pan over medium heat. Add the pine nuts and toast them gently, shaking the pan to cook them evenly. As soon as they turn golden brown, pour them into a bowl to stop the cooking.

Place the basil and garlic in a mortar and crush well. Add the pine nuts and crush them into the mixture. Mix in the grated cheese. Finally, add the olive oil in a thin stream, stirring constantly.

Alternatively, the basil and garlic can be blended in a food processor. Add the pine nuts and grated cheese and continue to mix all the ingredients in the machine. With the motor running, add the olive oil in a thin stream.

Pesto tastes as good warm as it does cold.

1. Heat a dry pan and add the pine nuts.

2. Toast the pine nuts.

3. Combine the basil and garlic in a mortar.

4. Mash it well.

5. Add the pine nuts, grated pecorino, and olive oil.

6. Blend well.

7. The pesto is ready to serve.

Pea sauce

This sauce suits warm fish dishes, pasta, and vegetables very well.

Makes 4 servings:

3 shallots
2 cloves garlic
2 tablespoons olive oil
½ cup Vegetable Stock (See recipe page 167)
10 oz green peas
½ teaspoon salt
½ teaspoon pepper
½ teaspoon sugar
1 tablespoon butter, cut into cubes (optional)

Preparation:
Peel and finely chop the shallots. Chop or crush the garlic in a mortar, if you like.

Heat the olive oil in a saucepan over medium-high heat. Add the shallots when the oil is warm and sauté until they are golden brown and tender. Meanwhile, heat the stock in a separate saucepan.

Pour the warm stock over the shallots. Add the garlic, peas, salt, pepper, and sugar and let it all sizzle, stirring constantly, for 3 minutes.

Blend everything together with a hand-held mixer. The sauce may be used now, if you like. Or, strain the mixture through a sieve into a new pan. Reheat, then stir in the cubes of butter with a spoon until melted and smooth. The sauce is ready to serve.

1. Sauté the shallots in olive oil.

2. Add the vegetable stock, peas, garlic, salt, pepper, and sugar. Blend it all together with a hand-held mixer.

3. Now the sauce has a full-bodied consistency and may be served at this point.

4. Or, press the sauce through a sieve and add butter.
This ready-to-serve sauce glistens nicely.

Red beet sauce

Red beet sauce complements fish, vegetables, and lentils nicely.

Makes 4 servings:
3 cooked red beets
3 shallots
2 tablespoons olive oil
1 whole clove
1 cinnamon stick
½ teaspoon salt
½ teaspoon pepper
1 cup Vegetable Stock (See recipe page 167)
1 tablespoon butter, cut into cubes

Preparation:
Cut the red beets into cubes. Peel and finely chop the shallots.

Heat the olive oil in a saucepan over medium heat. Add the shallots when the oil is warm. When the shallots are tender, add the red beet cubes, clove, cinnamon, salt, and pepper and let everything cook for 3 minutes.

Meanwhile, heat the vegetable stock, then pour it over the vegetables. Let it all simmer uncovered for 20 minutes, until the liquid reduces to one-quarter of the original amount.

Blend the mixture with a hand-held mixer and press it through a sieve into a new pan. Reheat, then stir in the butter with a spoon. The sauce is ready to serve.

Carrot jus

This sauce can be served with pasta or fish dishes.

Makes 4 servings:
2 shallots
2 carrots
1 knob fresh ginger
2 cloves garlic
2 tablespoons olive oil
½ teaspoon salt
½ teaspoon white pepper
½ teaspoon sugar
¾ cup Vegetable Stock (See recipe page 167)
1 tablespoon butter, cut into cubes

Preparation:
Peel and finely chop the shallots. Peel and wash the carrots, then dice them. Peel and finely chop the ginger. Crush the garlic. (Use a mortar, if you wish, and crush it together with the ginger.)

Heat the olive oil in a saucepan over medium-high heat. When it is hot, add the shallots and let them sizzle. When the shallots are tender, add the carrot cubes. Sprinkle in the salt, white pepper, and sugar while stirring. Turn the carrots and shallots over in the oil for at least 3 minutes. Add the ginger and garlic and continue to stir for another 1–2 minutes. Watch that they don't burn.

While the vegetables are sizzling in the olive oil, heat up the stock in another saucepan. Pour the warm stock over the vegetables, reduce the heat to medium, and simmer uncovered for 20 minutes, until the liquid has reduced to one-quarter of the original amount.

Blend the mixture with the hand-held mixer and press it through a sieve into a new pan. Rewarm the mixture, stir in the butter with a spoon, and the sauce is ready to serve.

Asparagus sauce

Asparagus sauce suits fish dishes and any pasta or rice dish.

Makes 4 servings:
3 shallots
15 asparagus spears
2 tablespoons olive oil
½ teaspoon salt
½ teaspoon pepper
½ cup Vegetable Stock (See recipe page 167)
1 tablespoon butter, cut into cubes

Preparation:
Peel and finely chop the shallots. Peel and trim the asparagus and cut it into small pieces.

Heat the olive oil in a saucepan over medium-high heat and when it is warm, add the shallots. Sauté the shallots until they are tender and golden brown. Add the asparagus with the salt and pepper and cook for 3 minutes.

While the vegetables are sizzling in the olive oil, heat up the vegetable stock in another saucepan. Pour the warm stock over the vegetables and cook uncovered for 5 minutes.

Blend the mixture with the hand-held mixer and press it through a sieve into a new pan. Reheat the mixture, then stir in the butter with a spoon. The sauce is ready to serve.

Cauliflower sauce

Cauliflower sauce pairs well with vegetables and warm meat or fish dishes.

Makes 4 servings:
3 shallots
1 small cauliflower
1 clove garlic
2 tablespoons olive oil
½ teaspoon salt
½ teaspoon white pepper
½ teaspoon sugar
1 cup Vegetable Stock (See recipe page 167)
1 tablespoon butter, cut into cubes

Preparation:
Peel and finely chop the shallots. Wash the cauliflower and cut into small florets. Peel and crush the garlic.

Heat the olive oil in a saucepan over medium-high heat and when it is warm, add the shallots. When the shallots are tender and golden brown, stir in the garlic, cauliflower, salt, white pepper, and sugar. Let everything cook for 3 minutes.

While the vegetables are sizzling in the oil, heat up the vegetable stock in another saucepan. Pour the warm stock over the vegetables and cook uncovered for 20 minutes, until the liquid has reduced to one-quarter of the original amount.

Blend the mixture with the hand-held mixer and press it through a sieve. Stir in the butter with a spoon. The sauce is ready to serve.

Tomato sauce

This tomato sauce has a broad range of uses: for meat and fish dishes, as well as salads, pasta, rice, and lentils.

Make 4 servings:
3 shallots
1 onion
2 cloves garlic
2 tablespoons olive oil
1 can (28 oz) crushed tomatoes
1 teaspoon dried oregano
1 tablespoon chopped fresh basil
½ teaspoon salt
½ teaspoon black pepper
½ teaspoon cayenne pepper
½ teaspoon sugar
3 tablespoons Vegetable Stock (See recipe page 167)

Preparation:
Peel and finely chop the shallots. Peel and finely chop the onion. Peel and crush the garlic, in a mortar if you wish.

Heat the olive oil in a saucepan over medium-high heat. When the oil is warm, add the shallots and onion. Cook until the onion and shallots are tender and golden brown. Add the garlic, tomato, herbs, spices, and sugar and let it all sizzle for 3 minutes.

Meanwhile, heat up the stock in another saucepan, then pour it over the vegetables. Cover and simmer for 1 hour, stirring occasionally.

The sauce is ready to serve.

Sauce périgueux

This luxurious truffle sauce is an excellent accompaniment to all grilled birds, such as chicken, pheasant, and duck.

Makes 4 servings:
3 cups Demi-glace (See recipe page 171)
6 tablespoons black truffle oil
3½ oz black truffles
½ teaspoon salt
½ teaspoon pepper

Preparation:
Heat the demi-glace to a boil over medium heat. Stir in the truffle oil and simmer for a few minutes. Mash the truffles with a fork and add them to the sauce. Set the pan aside and let settle for 10 minutes. Season with salt and pepper. The sauce is ready to serve.

White onion sauce

This simple sauce is good with cooked potatoes and smoked pork loin.

Makes 4 servings:
2 onions
2 tablespoons olive oil
2 tablespoons butter
2 tablespoons flour
3 cups milk
½ teaspoon salt
¼ teaspoon grated nutmeg
½ teaspoon cayenne pepper

Preparation:
Halve and peel the onions. Slice the halves into small wedges.

Heat the olive oil in a saucepan over medium-high heat. When the oil is hot, add the onions and sauté until they are golden brown and tender.

Add the butter to the pan. When the butter has melted, add the flour. Heat up the milk in another saucepan. Pour the warmed milk into the pan with the onion and butter, stirring constantly until the sauce thickens.

Add the salt, grated nutmeg, and cayenne pepper and let the sauce simmer for at least 10 minutes, stirring from time to time.

The sauce is ready to serve.

Fig sauce

Fig sauce is delicious with wild fowl, such as squab, pheasant, and thrush. The sauce may also be served with other meat courses and sautéed goose liver.

Makes 4 servings:
1 tablespoon butter
4 fresh figs
2 tablespoons honey
6 tablespoons sherry vinegar
6 tablespoons Chicken Jus (See recipe page 19)
½ teaspoon salt

Preparation:
Melt half of the butter in a pan over medium heat. Slice the figs into wedges and let them sizzle in the butter for about 5 minutes. Add the honey and let the fruit caramelize for 3–4 minutes with steady stirring. Now the fruit is glazed.

Add the vinegar and chicken jus and bring to a boil. Add salt and simmer for a few minutes.

Strain the sauce through a sieve into a new saucepan, pressing with a spoon so that most of the fruit flesh goes through the sieve.

Set the sauce over low heat and stir in the rest of the butter with a spoon. The sauce is ready to serve.

Apple sauce

Apple sauce is perfect with any pork dish, such as roast pork or grilled pork ribs. It is also very nice with chicken and veal.

Makes 4 servings:
2 apples
1 tablespoon butter
2 tablespoons honey
6 tablespoons sherry vinegar
6 tablespoons Veal Jus (See recipe page 26)
½ teaspoon salt

Preparation:
Core the apples and cut them into wedges. Melt half of the butter in a pan over medium heat. Add the apples and let them sizzle in the butter for about 5 minutes. Add the honey and let the fruit caramelize for 3–4 minutes, stirring constantly. Deglaze the pan by pouring in the vinegar and stirring as it fizzes in the pan. Simmer until the liquid is reduced by half.

Add the veal jus and bring the liquid to a boil. Season with salt and simmer for a few more minutes.

Strain the sauce through a sieve into a new saucepan, pressing with a spoon so that most of the fruit flesh goes through the sieve.

Set the sauce over low heat and stir in the rest of the butter with a spoon. The sauce is ready to serve.

Prune sauce

Prune sauce is an excellent match for all kinds of birds, veal, and pork.

Makes 4 servings:
1 tablespoon butter
12 pitted prunes
2 tablespoons honey
6 tablespoons sherry vinegar
6 tablespoons Chicken Jus (See recipe page 19)
½ teaspoon salt

Preparation:
Melt half of the butter in a pan over medium heat. Add the whole prunes and let them sizzle in the butter for about 5 minutes. Add the honey and let the fruit caramelize for 3–4 minutes, stirring constantly. Deglaze the pan by pouring in the vinegar and stirring as it fizzes in the pan. Simmer until the liquid is reduced by half.

Add the chicken jus and bring the liquid to a boil. Season with salt and simmer for a few more minutes.

Strain the sauce through a sieve into a new saucepan, pressing with a spoon so that most of the fruit flesh goes through the sieve.

Set the sauce over low heat, and stir in the rest of the butter with a spoon. The sauce is ready to serve.

Grape sauce

Grape sauce marries well with goose, duck, or chicken livers. Try it with a warm chicken liver salad.

Makes 4 servings:
1 tablespoon butter
20 grapes, preferably seedless
2 tablespoons honey
6 tablespoons sherry vinegar
6 tablespoons Chicken Jus (See recipe page 19)
½ teaspoon salt

Preparation:
Cut the grapes in half. Melt half of the butter in a pan over medium heat. Add the grapes and let them sizzle in the butter for about 5 minutes.

Add the honey and let the grapes caramelize for 3–4 minutes, stirring constantly. Deglaze the pan by pouring in the vinegar and stirring as it fizzes in the pan. Simmer until the liquid is reduced by half.

Add the chicken jus and bring the liquid to a boil. Season with salt and simmer for a few more minutes.

Strain the sauce through a sieve into a new saucepan, pressing with a spoon so that most of the fruit flesh goes through the sieve.

Set the sauce over low heat and stir in the rest of the butter with a spoon. The sauce is ready to serve.

Apricot sauce

This sauce is excellent for grilled, cooked, or panfried lamb or pork dishes.

Makes 4 servings:
1 tablespoon butter
8 dried apricots
2 tablespoons honey
6 tablespoons sherry vinegar
6 tablespoons Lamb Jus or Chicken Jus (See recipe page 11 or page 19)
½ teaspoon salt

Preparation:
Melt half of the butter in a pan over medium heat. Add the whole apricots and let them sizzle in the butter for about 5 minutes.

Add the honey and let the fruit caramelize for 3–4 minutes, stirring constantly. Deglaze the pan by pouring in the vinegar and stirring as it fizzes in the pan. Simmer until the liquid is reduced by half.

Add lamb jus and bring the liquid to a boil. Season with salt and simmer for a few minutes more.

Pour the sauce through a sieve into a new pan, pressing and smearing with the back of a spoon so that most of the fruit flesh goes through the sieve.

Set the sauce over low heat and stir in the rest of the butter with a spoon. The sauce is ready to serve.

Chèvre-filled ravioli in tomato sauce

Makes 4 servings:

Pasta:
2½ cups flour
3 eggs
3 tablespoons olive oil
½ teaspoon salt
2 teaspoons water

Filling:
10 oz chèvre
5 tablespoons olive oil
2 tablespoons finely grated Parmesan

1 whisked egg

Garnish:
Warm Tomato Sauce (See recipe page 120)
Fresh flat-leaf parsley
Snipped fresh chives
Shaved Parmesan

Preparation:
To make the pasta, mix flour, egg, olive oil, salt, and water in a bowl. Knead the dough into a firm lump. Cut the dough into 6 equal parts and wrap each piece in plastic wrap. Let the pieces rest in the refrigerator for at least 2 hours before use.

To make the filling, mix the chèvre, olive oil, and Parmesan in a food processor.

Take the pasta dough pieces from the refrigerator one at a time. Roll the dough out ¹⁄₁₆ inch thick. Cut into 4-by-2-inch pieces. Add a little filling to one side of each piece.

Brush the border of each piece with the whisked egg and glue each ravioli pillow closed. The ravioli can be cooked as is, or you can use a small cookie cutter to trim them into decorative round shapes.

Gently boil the ravioli for 3 minutes. Serve the pasta with warm tomato sauce, garnished with parsley, chives, and Parmesan.

Dips

Dips are simple and quick to prepare and make a great accompaniment to grilled meats, salty snacks, and raw vegetables.

Horseradish dip

This dip has zing! It's delicious with raw vegetables, grilled or fried meats, or fried potatoes.

Makes 4 servings:

½ cup crème fraîche
¾ oz prepared horseradish or ½ cup grated fresh horseradish
½ teaspoon salt

Preparation:
Mix the crème fraîche in a bowl with the horseradish and salt. Serve.

1. Place the horseradish, salt, and crème fraîche
in a bowl. Mix well and serve.

Avocado dip

This avocado dip is delicious as a topping on toast with hard-boiled egg or with cold shellfish like shrimp or lobster. It's also excellent with raw vegetables or tortilla chips.

Makes 4 servings:

4 avocados
Juice of 1½ lemons
¼ cup crème fraîche
½ teaspoon salt
½ teaspoon cayenne pepper

Preparation:
Pit the avocados, reserving 1 pit, and scoop the flesh into a bowl. Mash the avocado flesh and add lemon juice, crème fraîche, salt, and cayenne pepper. Mix well.

Place the avocado pit in the center of the dip. The pit, along with the lemon juice, will help the dip keep its color longer.

1. Mash the avocado with a fork and
add the lemon juice.

2. Add the crème fraîche, salt, and cayenne pepper.

3. Mix well.
Serve the dip at once so it doesn't turn brown.

Garlic dip

Garlic dip is great for raw vegetables, baked potatoes, and of course, potato chips. It's also good with cold and warm meat and fish dishes.

Makes 4 servings:
½ cup crème fraîche
2 crushed garlic cloves
½ teaspoon salt
½ teaspoon pepper
¼ teaspoon cayenne pepper

Preparation:
Place the crème fraîche in a bowl. Add the garlic. Season with salt, pepper, and cayenne pepper. Serve.

Herb dip

This dip tastes wonderful with deep-fried vegetables and fish, but can also be served with raw vegetables. It's especially good with radishes. The herbs have to be fresh.

Makes 4 servings:
½ cup crème fraîche
2 tablespoons chopped flat-leaf parsley
2 tablespoons chopped tarragon
2 tablespoons chopped chervil
2 tablespoons chopped chives
½ tablespoon chopped rosemary
½ tablespoon chopped thyme
¼ teaspoon cayenne pepper
Juice of ½ lemon
½ teaspoon salt
½ teaspoon pepper

Preparation:
Place the crème fraîche in a bowl and add all of the chopped herbs. Add the cayenne, stir in the lemon juice, and season with salt and pepper. Serve.

Roquefort dip

You must try this dip with raw celery sticks. It may also be served with potato chips, sliced and toasted baguette, or melba toasts.

Makes 4 servings:
6 tablespoons crème fraîche
5 oz Roquefort
½ teaspoon salt
½ teaspoon pepper
10 drops Tabasco
2 tablespoons chopped chives

Preparation:
Place the crème fraîche in a bowl and mash in the Roquefort with a fork. Season the dip with salt, pepper, and Tabasco. Add the chopped chives and serve.

Yogurt dip

This is a light and fresh dip, nice with grilled eggplant or raw cucumber. It can also be used as a dressing for a salad made with bitter greens, such as arugula or frisée, or it may be served with grilled chicken.

Makes 4 servings:
½ cup plain yogurt
1 clove garlic, crushed
2 tablespoons chopped parsley
2 tablespoons chopped chives
½ teaspoon salt
½ teaspoon pepper
½ teaspoon sugar
1 teaspoon sherry vinegar

Preparation:
Place the yogurt in a bowl and add the crushed garlic and chopped herbs. Season with salt, pepper, sugar, and sherry vinegar. Serve.

Vegetables with herb dip

Makes 4 servings:

1 cucumber
12 pieces Tomato Confit (See recipe
page 177)
1 fennel bulb
3 carrots
4 oz haricots verts, cooked
3 celery stalks
Herb Dip (See recipe page 138)

Preparation:
Wash all the vegetables and cut them into
sticks. Arrange the vegetables on a platter
with a generous amount of dip.

In addition to the ingredients mentioned in
this recipe, the dip is a good accompaniment
to many other kinds of vegetables, such as red
and black radish, asparagus, all kinds of beans,
rutabaga, cauliflower, and turnips.

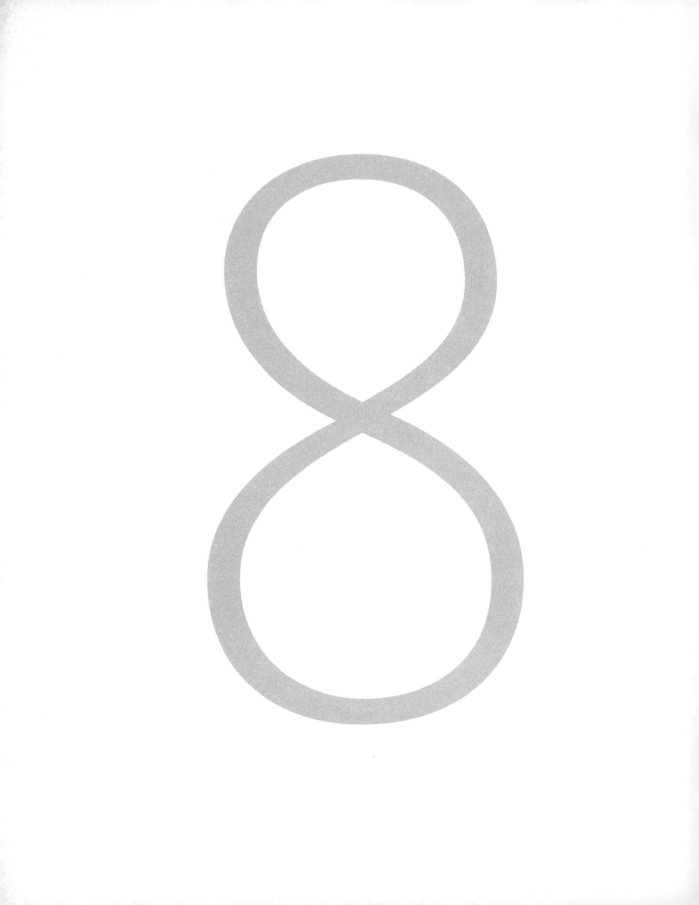

Salsas

Salsa is the Spanish word for sauce, particularly used to designate the spicy, vegetable-based sauces common to Latin American kitchens. Salsas often have a chunky consistency and are served cold or lukewarm.

Olive salsa

Olive salsa can be served on toast or used as a pizza topping. The salsa can also be used on salad.

Makes 4 servings:

1 clove garlic
5 tablespoons coarsely chopped
black olives
5 tablespoons coarsely chopped
green olives
2 tablespoons finely chopped
flat-leaf parsley
2 tablespoons olive oil
1 tablespoon coarsely chopped caper
berries or capers

Preparation:
Crush the garlic in a mortar.

Mix all the ingredients well. Refrigerate the salsa for 1 hour before serving.

1. Crush the garlic in a mortar.

2. Add the coarsely chopped olives, capers, and flat-leaf parsley.

3. Stir in the olive oil and serve.

Tomato salsa

Versatile tomato salsa complements grilled foods, salads, and of course tortilla chips.

Makes 4 servings:

8 tomatoes
1 clove garlic
2 tablespoons finely chopped red onion
1 teaspoon sugar
1 tablespoon olive oil
½ teaspoon cayenne pepper
1 tablespoon finely chopped chives
1 tablespoon finely chopped flat-leaf parsley
½ teaspoon salt

Preparation:
Score a cross on the top of each tomato. Place the tomatoes in boiling water for 1½ minutes and transfer them directly to an ice-water bath. Halve the tomatoes, discard the seeds, and cut the rest of the flesh into cubes.

Crush the garlic in a mortar.

Mix all the ingredients together thoroughly. Refrigerate the salsa for 1 hour before serving.

1. Crush the garlic in a mortar.

2. Combine all the ingredients.

3. Mix thoroughly, chill, and serve.

Pepper salsa

This salsa can be served on top of toast or as a side to grilled fish.

Makes 4 servings:
1 red bell pepper
1 yellow bell pepper
1 green bell pepper
1 red chile
2 tablespoons finely chopped cilantro
1 tablespoon finely chopped chives
1 tablespoon ground cumin
2 tablespoons olive oil
1 tablespoon sherry vinegar
½ teaspoon salt

Preparation:
Preheat the oven to 350°F. Place the whole bell peppers on a baking sheet and bake for 10–15 minutes, turning once or twice, until they begin to char.

Take out the peppers and place them in a bowl of ice water to stop the cooking.

Peel the peppers. The skins should be loose enough to slip off easily. Halve the peppers, remove the stem and seeds, and cut the flesh into cubes.

Cut the chile in half, remove the stem and seeds, and finely chop the rest. For a spicier salsa, leave some of the seeds.

Mix the peppers and the chopped chile in a bowl. Add the remaining ingredients and mix well. Refrigerate the salsa for at least 1 hour before serving.

Salsa verde

Try this with all types of fish dishes, especially with grilled fish.

Makes 4 servings:
4 tablespoons finely chopped flat-leaf parsley
2 tablespoons finely chopped chervil
2 tablespoons finely chopped cilantro
1 teaspoon finely chopped capers
Juice of 1 lemon
3 tablespoons olive oil

Preparation:
Mix all the ingredients together well. Refrigerate the salsa for 1 hour before serving.

Eggplant salsa

Serve eggplant salsa with grilled lamb or grilled chicken. It also tastes wonderful on toast.

Makes 4 servings:
2 eggplants
¼ cup olive oil
½ teaspoon salt
1 clove garlic, crushed
½ teaspoon curry powder
½ teaspoon ground cumin
1 tablespoon finely chopped cilantro
1 tablespoon finely chopped flat-leaf parsley
½ teaspoon pepper

Preparation:
Cut the eggplant into ½-inch-thick slices and then into cubes.

Heat half of the olive oil in a sauté pan over medium-high heat. When the oil is smoking hot, add the eggplant pieces. Sprinkle with the salt and fry the eggplant pieces until they are tender and golden brown.

Transfer the warm eggplant to a bowl and mix with the crushed garlic, curry, and cumin.

When the mixture has cooled, add the remaining ingredients along with the rest of the oil. Mix well and refrigerate for 1 hour before serving.

Squash salsa

This salsa is perfect for topping a tomato salad or as a complement to grilled foods.

Makes 4 servings:
1 yellow squash
1 zucchini
3 tablespoons olive oil
2 cloves garlic
1 tablespoon finely chopped thyme
½ teaspoon pepper
2 tablespoons grated Parmesan
1 tablespoon finely chopped chervil
Juice of 1 lemon

Preparation:
Cut the squash and zucchini into slices and then in cubes.

Heat half of the olive oil in a sauté pan over medium-high heat. When the oil is smoking hot, add the squash and zucchini. Fry the squash for 1½ minutes, until al dente.

Crush the garlic in a mortar into a paste, then add it to the pan along with the thyme and pepper. Mix everything thoroughly before transferring it to a serving bowl. When the mixture has cooled, added the Parmesan, chervil, and lemon juice. Stir in the rest of the oil and refrigerate for 1 hour before serving.

Foundation recipes

Good basics ensure that a finished sauce has full flavor and the right consistency. It's time consuming to make some of the stocks, but remember that you can make large quantities and freeze them in portions.

Mussel stock

To make a mussel stock, start with fresh mussels and cook them yourself. The stock may be served as is, alongside the mussels, or it can be used as a base for fish sauce, soups, and fish casseroles.

Makes 4 servings:

5 lb fresh mussels
5 shallots
2 stems flat-leaf parsley
2 tablespoons olive oil
1½ cups white wine
½ teaspoon salt
½ teaspoon pepper
6 tablespoons butter
6 tablespoons heavy cream (optional)

Preparation:
Scrape the mussels clean and remove any beards. Rinse under cold running water or soak in cold water for 2 hours, changing water frequently, so that all the sand is cleaned away. Strain the mussels and shake the water off. Throw away any mussels whose shells are open or damaged. Set aside.

Peel and finely chop the shallots. Wash the parsley and pluck the leaves. Finely chop the leaves and reserve the stems.

Heat the olive oil in a large pan over medium-high heat. Add the shallots and parsley stems. Sizzle for 1 minute. Add the mussels. Stir for 2–3 minutes, until the mussel shells begin to get hot. Add the white wine and the butter. Sprinkle in the chopped parsley. Cover, bring to a boil, and cook for 5–6 minutes, stirring occasionally.

If the mussels are to be served, remove and discard the parsley stems and any mussels that have not opened.

To further refine the stock, pour the liquid through a sieve into a new pan. Set aside the mussels in the sieve. Let the stock simmer until the liquid is reduced by half. Add 6 tablespoons of heavy cream and boil for another 2 minutes, stirring. The stock will turn into a beautiful creamy mussel sauce. Season the sauce with salt and pepper, and serve.

1. Sauté the shallots and parsley stems in olive oil.
Add the mussels.

2. Add the white wine and butter.

3. Sprinkle the chopped parsley over the top.

4. Strain the stock.

5. Season with salt and pepper. For a creamy variation, reduce the liquid by half.
Add heavy cream, simmer, and the sauce is ready to serve.

Vegetable stock

You can use vegetable stock instead of chicken stock as an all-purpose base for sauces and soups, or for cooking vegetables.

Makes 8 cups:

1 onion
1 leek
2 peeled carrots
2 celery stalks
1 Bouquet Garni (See recipe page 175)
1 tablespoon coarse salt
1½ tablespoons whole black peppercorns

Preparation:
Cut the onion, leek, carrots, and celery into large pieces. Place the vegetables and bouquet garni in a pot. Pour in just enough cold water to cover all the vegetables, and add the salt and peppercorns.

Bring to a simmer over medium heat and let cook for 2½ hours. Don't stir while the mixture is simmering. If foam forms on the surface, remove it carefully with a skimmer.

When the mixture has finished cooking, strain and let cool at room temperature. The stock can be stored in the refrigerator for up to 24 hours. If you want to store it longer, it can be frozen. In this case it should be frozen directly after it has cooled.

1. Place the coarsely cut vegetables and bouquet garni in a pot. Cover with water.

2. After the vegetables have boiled, strain the stock.

3. Season with salt and pepper if desired,
and the stock is ready.

Chicken stock

Chicken stock is the stock I use the most. It is an excellent flavor booster and can be used both for soups and sauces. It can also be used for cooking vegetables.

Makes 8 cups:
6 lb chicken carcasses
2 onions
1 leek
2 peeled carrots
2 celery stalks
4 stems flat-leaf parsley
1 tablespoon coarse salt
1½ tablespoons whole black peppercorns

Preparation:
Place the carcasses in a stockpot and cover with cold water. Bring to a boil with the lid on. Remove the lid and boil rapidly for 5 minutes. Pour out the liquid and discard. Rinse the carcasses. (This process is called blanching, and it removes impurities from the carcasses.)

While the carcasses blanch, cut the onion, leek, carrots, and celery into big pieces. Add the vegetables and parsley to the pot with the blanched chicken carcasses and pour in just enough fresh cold water to cover the ingredients. Add the salt and peppercorns.

Bring to a simmer over medium heat and let cook for 2½ hours. Don't stir while the mixture is simmering. If foam forms on the surface, remove it carefully with a skimmer.

When the mixture has finished cooking, strain and let cool at room temperature. Note that chicken stock should have a neutral taste. The stock can be stored in the refrigerator for up to 24 hours. If you want to store it longer, it can be frozen. In this case it should be frozen directly after it has cooled.

Veal stock and demi-glace

Veal stock and demi-glace can be used as the base for sauces and braises of meat, fish, and vegetables. First you make a veal stock. If you then reduce this stock to half the original amount, it is called demi-glace. While the demi-glace is warm, it has the consistency of syrup; when cold, it jells. It's most practical to prepare the demi-glace in large portions and then freeze it in small portions to use as needed.

Makes 8 cups demi-glace:
10 lb veal bones, with joints and marrow
2–3 tablespoons olive oil
1 onion
1 whole garlic head
3 tomatoes
2 carrots
1 whole bunch celery, leaves removed
8 mushrooms
1½ gallons (24 cups/6 qt) cold water
4 tablespoons tomato paste
1½ tablespoons coarse salt
1½ tablespoons whole black peppercorns

Preparation:
Preheat the oven to 425°F. Place the bones in a roasting pan and drizzle with 2–3 tablespoons oil. Roast the bones until browned, about 30 minutes, turning the bones 2 or 3 times to brown evenly. This process will determine the color of the finished stock.

Wash, trim, and cut the vegetables into large pieces while the veal bones are in the oven. When the veal bones are browned, add the vegetables to the pan. Let everything continue to brown for another 30 minutes. Stir the mixture every 10 minutes to prevent burning. If the ingredients are burned, the finished stock will have an unpleasant bitter flavor.

When the ingredients are completely browned, place the bones and vegetables in a large stockpot. (Leave the rendered fat behind in the roasting pan, and discard). Pour in just enough of the water to cover the ingredients. Add the tomato paste, salt, and peppercorns. Simmer for 6 hours, uncovered, adding more water as needed to keep the ingredients covered. Remove the foam carefully with a skimmer as it comes to the surface of the liquid.

Strain the liquid through a sieve when it is finished cooking. The veal stock is ready to use. Because it contains natural gelatin from the bones, the stock will congeal when it is cooled.

To make demi-glace, let the strained liquid reduce until there are approximately 8 cups remaining. To prevent stock from congealing on the sides of the pot, brush the sides occasionally with water.

The veal stock or demi-glace can be stored in the refrigerator for up to 24 hours. If you want to store it longer, it can be divided into small portions and frozen. In this case it should be frozen directly after it has cooled.

Fish stock

Fish stock can be used as a base for fish soup, as a seafood braise, or for cooking shellfish. Fish stock can also be used as a base for fish velouté, which is a creamy fish stock thickened with a flour and butter roux.

Makes 2 cups:
3 carrots
2 onions
2 shallots
3 tablespoons olive oil
1 lb rinsed fish bones from white fish
5 flat-leaf parsley stems with leaves
1 bay leaf
1 tablespoon whole black peppercorn
1 tablespoon coarse salt

Preparation:
Wash, trim, and coarsely chop the vegetables. Heat the olive oil in a pot over medium heat and add the vegetables. Sauté for 4–5 minutes without letting the vegetables brown. Add the fish bones and let them sizzle for 3–4 minutes more.

Pour in just enough fresh cold water to cover the ingredients. Add the parsley, bay leaf, and peppercorns. Bring to a boil and let simmer, uncovered, for 20 minutes. Do not let the liquid boil rapidly, or the stock will turn cloudy.

After 20 minutes of simmering, add the salt. Set stock aside for 5 minutes and then strain it through a sieve.

The stock can be stored in the refrigerator for up to 24 hours. If you want to store it longer, it can be frozen.

Lobster bouillon

Lobster bouillon can be used for cooking fish or vegetables, or as a base for lobster velouté and fish soups. It can also be served as is, adding lobster tail meat, 1 teaspoon crème fraîche, and garnishing with caviar or seaweed.

Makes 4 cups:
2 live lobsters, about ¾ lb each
(or frozen lobster)
1 onion
1 shallot
1 whole garlic head
2 tomatoes
3 tablespoons olive oil
½ cup white wine
2 tablespoons cognac
1 tablespoon coarse salt
2 tablespoons whole black peppercorns

Preparation:
Fill a large pot with water and bring to a boil over high heat. Plunge the lobsters into the boiling water, cover, return to a boil, and cook for 20 seconds before transferring them to a platter. Reserve 6 cups of the water.

Break off the lobster tails and claws. (These are the choicest parts of the lobster and too delicate to use in a stock. Cook the tail and claw meat until it is opaque throughout, remove the dark vein from the tail, and use in a salad or soup or as a dish in itself.)

Divide the lobster bodies in two lengthwise. Remove the stomach sac, eyes, and antennae and discard. Using a hammer, break up the shells. Blend the rest of the lobster, including the shell, in a food processor to a pureelike consistency.

Finely chop the onion and shallot. Coarsely chop the garlic. Wash the tomatoes, core, and cut into quarters.

Heat the olive oil over medium-high heat in a pot with the capacity to add at least 8 cups of liquid. Add the lobster puree and let it sizzle for a few minutes. Add the shallot, onion, and garlic. Let sizzle for 1 minute. Add the tomatoes. Mix well and simmer for 30 seconds.

Add white wine and cognac at the same time. The mixture should reduce until the liquid has almost all evaporated. Add the reserved 6 cups lobster-cooking water. Add the salt and peppercorns and simmer for 35 minutes. Remove from the heat, cover, and let the bouillon stand for 10 minutes. Strain the mixture through a fine sieve, pressing with the back of a spoon to extract all the liquid, as this is where the flavor is concentrated. The bouillon is ready to use.

Bouquet garni

Bouquet garni is a very versatile flavor booster, used in many stocks, jus, soups, and sauces. In the classical French kitchen, the bouquet garni is comprised of the following vegetables and herbs:

Bay leaf
Thyme
Celery stalk
Flat-leaf parsley
Leek

Preparation:
Pack all the ingredients into the leek, wrap with kitchen string, and tie tightly. The bouquet garni is ready to use.

Grilled halibut with creamy mussel stock

Makes 4 servings:
8 baby fennel bulbs (or 2 regular bulbs cut into 4 pieces each)
2 zucchini
8 asparagus spears
2 tablespoons olive oil
½ teaspoon salt
½ teaspoon pepper
½ cup Chicken Stock (See recipe page 170)
5 cloves garlic, crushed
1 tablespoon butter
1½ lb halibut filets
16 thin slices Tomato Confit
(See recipe opposite)
5 basil stems with leaves
¾ cup Mussel Stock (See recipe page 159)

Preparation:
Wash and trim the fennel and zucchini and cut the zucchini into ⅜ inch slices. Snap woody ends off asparagus spears.

Heat the olive oil in a pan over medium-high heat. Add the fennel, asparagus, and squash, season with the salt and pepper, and sizzle for 2 minutes. Bring the chicken stock to a boil in a separate pan. Pour the boiling stock over the vegetables to just cover them.

Add the crushed garlic to the vegetables and stock. Add the butter, cover, and simmer for 3 minutes.

Remove the squash and the asparagus and set aside. Cover the pan and cook the fennel for an additional 3 minutes.

Meanwhile, prepare a grill for direct cooking over medium-high heat, or, just before the vegetables are finished cooking, heat a grill pan over high heat. Brush a little oil on both sides of the fish and sprinkle with salt and pepper to taste. Place the fish on the grill or place it in the pan over high heat, then turn down the heat to medium-high. Cook the fish, turning once, until it has a nice golden brown color on each side. Let the fish rest for a few minutes, preferably on a rack, before serving.

Arrange the vegetables on serving plates, tucking in the pieces of tomato confit. Pluck the basil leaves and sprinkle them over the vegetables. Place the halibut filets on the plates and top with creamy mussel stock.

This dish can also be prepared with other types of fish, like sea catfish, arctic char, or mackerel.

Tomato confit

These tender, sweet oven-dried tomatoes can
be served as a dish on their own, in salads, or
as a garnish for meat and fish. This dish is best
prepared during the summer when sun-ripened
tomatoes are available.

Makes 48 tomato pieces:
12 ripe tomatoes
6 cloves garlic
1½ tablespoons coarse salt
½ teaspoon sugar
1 tablespoon ground white pepper
3 thyme stems
6 tablespoons olive oil, plus more to store

Preparation:
Bring a pot of water to a boil. Score a small cross
in the top of each tomato. Plunge them into
the boiling water for 20 seconds. Transfer them
directly into a bowl of cold water to stop the
cooking, then peel off the skins.

Preheat the oven to 125°F and line a baking
sheet with parchment paper or aluminum foil.
Cut the tomatoes into quarters and remove
the seeds. Peel the garlic. Arrange the tomato
pieces on the pan spacing evenly. Add the salt,
sugar, white pepper, whole garlic cloves, and
thyme stems. Drizzle olive oil over everything.

Bake the tomatoes on the middle rack of the
oven for 4 hours. The tomato confit can be put
in a jar and covered with olive oil to store for
10–15 days. Tomato confit should not be frozen.

Grilled halibut with creamy mussel stock

Spirit-based sauces

Spirit-based sauces enhance rich meat dishes. They require skill to make, but reward it with unparalleled depth of flavor.

Madeira sauce

This sauce is traditionally served with sautéed veal, but is also delicious with beef or chicken. Make this sauce in the same pan used to cook the meat.

Make 4 servings:

3 shallots
1½ tablespoons butter
¾ cup Madeira
¾ cup Demi-glace (See recipe page 171)
½ teaspoons salt
½ teaspoon ground white pepper
2 tablespoons crème fraîche (optional)

Preparation:
Brown the meat on all sides in the same pan you intend to use to make the sauce. Transfer the meat to a platter. The residue left in the pan will be the base for the sauce. (In French, this flavor concentrate is called the *suc.*)

Peel and finely chop the shallots. Place the pan used to cook the meat over medium-high heat and add half of the butter and the shallots. Sauté the shallots until golden brown and tender. This process will loosen the drippings and flavor and color the shallots.

Pour in the madeira and simmer until the liquid is reduced to one-quarter of the original amount. Add the demi-glace and boil for another 3–4 minutes. Season with salt and pepper.

Remove the pan from the heat and stir in the rest of the butter with a spoon. Strain the sauce and serve.

For a creamy variation, stir in the crème fraîche just before serving.

1. Sauté the shallots in the pan used to brown the meat.
Pour in the Madeira.

2. Add the demi-glace and simmer.

3. Season with the salt and pepper, and stir in the butter.

4. Strain the sauce and serve.

Cognac sauce

This cognac sauce is a delicious accompaniment to all types of poultry, from chicken and duck to squab and pheasant. If the chicken jus in the recipe is replaced with demi-glace, it complements lamb, beef, pork, or veal.

Makes 4 servings:

6 oz mushrooms
3 shallots
2 tablespoons olive oil
½ teaspoon salt
½ teaspoon pepper
3 tablespoons cognac
3 tablespoons white wine
2 cups Chicken Jus (See recipe page 19)
1 tablespoon butter
1 tablespoon finely chopped tarragon
1 tablespoon finely chopped chervil

Preparation:
Clean the mushrooms with a brush and slice them. Peel and finely chop the shallots.

Heat the olive oil in a heavy stainless-steel or enameled cast-iron pan. When the olive oil is smoking hot, add the mushrooms. Sprinkle in the salt and pepper and brown the mushrooms well. Add the shallots and let sizzle until the shallots are golden brown and tender.

Pour in the cognac and immediately light with a match to flambé the mushrooms and shallots. Let the flame extinguish on its own. Add the white wine. Simmer until the liquid is reduced to one-quarter of the original amount.

Add the chicken jus and let simmer for 2–3 minutes. Strain the sauce through a sieve. Stir in the butter with a spoon, and add the finely chopped herbs just before serving.

1. Brown the mushrooms, and add the shallots.

2. Pour in the cognac and immediately light
with a match.

3. Add the white wine.

4. Add the chicken jus.   5. Simmer.   6. Strain the sauce.

7. Stir in the butter and herbs and serve.

Sauce diablo

Sauce diablo is an excellent accompaniment to pork dishes, and can also be used for grilled lamb and beef.

Makes 4 servings:
½ cup dry white wine
1 tablespoon red wine vinegar
1 tablespoon finely chopped shallot
2 stems thyme
1 bay leaf
1 teaspoon coarse black pepper
¾ cup Demi-glace (See recipe page 171)
1 tablespoon butter
1 tablespoon finely chopped
flat-leaf parsley

Preparation:
Pour the white wine into a pan and bring to a boil over high heat. Add the vinegar, shallot, thyme, bay leaf, and pepper. Reduce the heat and simmer until the liquid is reduced to one-quarter of the original amount. Add the demi-glace and simmer for 3–4 minutes.

Strain the sauce through a sieve and bring the strained liquid to a boil. Remove from the heat and stir in the butter with a spoon. (If you use a whisk, the sauce will become too airy.) Stir in the flat-leaf parsley and serve.

Cumberland sauce

Despite its popularity in the English region of the same name, Cumberland sauce was invented in Germany. Serve it with game dishes.

Makes 4 servings:
1 orange
1 lemon
2 tablespoons olive oil
1 tablespoon finely chopped shallot
1 tablespoon Dijon mustard
¾ cup lingonberry or cranberry jam or jelly
6 tablespoons port
1 teaspoon salt
½ teaspoon cayenne pepper
½ teaspoon ground ginger

Preparation:
Peel the orange and lemon. Squeeze the juice from them and reserve. Cut both the orange and lemon peel into thin julienne strips. Blanch then by putting the strips in a pan of water, bringing it to a boil, then draining, changing the water, and repeating the process. This eliminates the bitter taste in the peel.

Heat the olive oil in a saucepan and, when it is hot, add the shallot. Let the shallot sizzle until it is golden and tender.

Add the orange and lemon peel to the pan and stir in the mustard. Mix well. Add the jam and stir until dissolved. Pour in the port and the orange and lemon juices, stirring constantly. Season with the salt, cayenne pepper, and ginger. Simmer, uncovered, for about 10 minutes, until the liquid is reduced by one-quarter and serve.

Tarragon sauce

This is an old-fashioned sauce that many people like to serve with beef. Tarragon sauce is also well suited to lamb and to cold and hot fish dishes.

Makes 4 servings:
½ cup fresh tarragon
6 tablespoons white wine
¾ cup Demi-glace (See recipe page 171)
1 tablespoon butter

Preparation:
Coarsely chop the tarragon. Reserve 1 tablespoon and place the rest in a pan. Add the white wine and bring to a boil over high heat. Reduce the heat and simmer until the liquid is reduced by half. Add the demi-glace and continue to simmer for 2–3 minutes longer.

Strain the mixture through a fine sieve into a clean pan. Rewarm it, remove from the heat, and carefully stir in the butter with a spoon. Add the remaining tarragon and serve.

Port wine sauce

Port wine sauce is ideal for foie gras, pâtés, squab, and hot chicken dishes. Because this sauce is sweet, it also makes a nice complement to sautéed fruit, such as apples or grapes, or even to pan-fried vegetables.

Makes 4 servings:
2 carrots
1 onion
4 shallots
2 tablespoons olive oil
1½ tablespoons cold butter
3 tablespoons port
3 tablespoons Demi-glace
(See recipe page 171)
½ teaspoon salt
½ teaspoon pepper
2 tablespoons crème fraîche (optional)

Preparation:
Wash and peel the carrots and peel the onion and shallots. Cut the carrots into small dice and finely chop the onion and shallots.

Heat the olive oil and half of the butter in a pan over medium heat. Add the vegetables and sauté until tender, but don't let them color. Add the port and simmer until the liquid is reduced by one-quarter.

Add the demi-glace and simmer for another 4–5 minutes. Season with the salt and pepper. Strain the sauce into a clean pan. Rewarm it, remove from the heat, and carefully stir in the butter with a spoon. Continue to stir the butter until totally melted. (The butter gives the sauce a shiny appearance and full flavor.)

For a creamy variation, stir in the crème fraîche just before serving.

Sauce chateaubriand

This sauce is suitable for beef or veal roasts.

Makes 4 servings:
6 tablespoons white wine
1 tablespoon finely chopped shallot
1 tablespoon finely chopped mushroom
1 cup Demi-glace (See recipe page 171)
1 tablespoon finely chopped tarragon
1 tablespoon finely chopped
flat-leaf parsley
6 tablespoons butter
1 tablespoon cold Herb Butter
(See recipe page 96)
Juice of ½ lemon
¼ teaspoon cayenne pepper
½ teaspoon salt

Preparation:
Mix the white wine, shallot, and mushroom in a pan. Bring to a boil over medium-high heat and simmer until the liquid is reduced by half. Add the demi-glace and simmer until reduced by half again.

Remove the pan from the heat and stir in the tarragon, parsley, and plain butter. Then, mount the sauce with the herb butter: Cut the herb butter into small pieces and stir them in one by one with a spoon. This gives the sauce a full-bodied consistency. Add the lemon juice, season with the cayenne pepper and salt, and serve.

Sauce chasseur

Rich sauce chasseur, also referred to as hunter's sauce, is delicious with all types of game.

Makes 4 servings:
3 tablespoons cold butter
6 oz wild mushrooms, thinly sliced
2 tablespoons finely chopped shallot
6 tablespoons white wine
3 tablespoons cognac
1½ cups Demi-glace (See recipe page 171)
1 tablespoon finely chopped tarragon
1 tablespoon finely chopped chervil
1 tablespoon finely chopped
flat-leaf parsley
½ teaspoon salt
½ teaspoon pepper

Preparation:
Melt 1 tablespoon of the butter in a pan over medium-high heat and add the mushrooms and shallot. Sauté until golden brown. Add the white wine and simmer until the liquid is reduced by half. Pour in the cognac and light immediately with a match. Let the flame extinguish on its own.

Add the demi-glace and simmer the mixture for 15 minutes.

Remove from the heat. Mount the sauce with the remaining 2 tablespoons butter: Cut the butter into small cubes and stir them in one by one with a spoon. This gives the sauce a full-bodied consistency.

Add the finely chopped herbs, season with the salt and pepper, and serve.

Champagne sauce

Serve champagne sauce with all types of fish and shellfish. This version is based on crayfish, but can also be made with lobster or white fish trimmings. Serve this dish along with fresh country bread to soak up every last drop.

Makes 4 servings:
5 tablespoons olive oil
3 lb live crayfish
3 cloves garlic
10 stems flat-leaf parsley
1 bottle champagne
1²⁄₃ cup cold butter
½ teaspoon salt
½ teaspoon pepper

Preparation:
Heat the olive oil over high heat in a large pot that is wider than it is tall. Put the crayfish in the pot when the olive oil is smoking hot. The crayfish will rapidly change color and turn red.

Coarsely chop the garlic and parsley leaves and add them to the pot of crayfish. Simmer for 2 minutes, stirring constantly. Make sure the garlic doesn't burn, to prevent a bitter flavor in the finished sauce.

Pour in the champagne and simmer until the liquid is reduced by half.

Cut the cold butter into cubes, whisk in one by one until the butter is melted. Boil for an additional 2–3 minutes, until the crayfish are opaque throughout. Season with salt and pepper, and serve in shallow bowls so that the crayfish are bathed in their own sauce.

Pepper sauce

This rich and creamy sauce is a delicious accompaniment to grilled steak or chicken.

Makes 4 servings:
1 tablespoon butter
1 tablespoon olive oil
6 tablespoons whole green peppercorns
3 tablespoons cognac
6 tablespoons white wine
6 tablespoons Demi-glace (See recipe page 171)
3 tablespoons crème fraîche
½ teaspoon salt

Preparation:
Put the butter and olive oil in a pan, add the peppercorns, and place over medium heat. When the peppercorns are hot, add the cognac and immediately light with a match. Let the flame extinguish on its own.

Add the white wine and simmer until the liquid is reduced by half. Stir in the demi-glace and simmer again until reduced by half.

Stir in the crème fraîche, season with the salt, and serve. For a milder sauce, you can strain the peppercorns from the sauce before serving.

Bordelaise

Bordelaise is a classic red wine sauce, suitable to be served with grilled meat or with game dishes.

Makes 4 servings:
4 cups water
1½ teaspoons salt
2 lbs cleaned marrow bones, cut 2 inches thick by the butcher
2 tablespoons olive oil
3 finely chopped shallots
½ teaspoon pepper
¾ cup red wine
1 stem thyme
1 bay leaf
1 bunch flat-leaf parsley
¾ cup Demi-glace (See recipe page 171)
2 tablespoons cold butter

Preparation:
Bring the water to a boil and add 1 teaspoon of the salt. When the water boils, add the marrow bones and boil for 1½ minutes. Take the bones out of the water and push the marrow from the bones. Cut the marrow into pieces, put them on a plate, and set aside.

Heat the olive oil in a heavy stainless-steel pan over medium heat. When the oil is hot, add the shallots, ½ teaspoon salt, and the pepper. Stir until the shallots are soft and tender without letting them turn brown.

Add the wine, thyme, bay leaf, and flat-leaf parsley bunch, after reserving 10 stems. Simmer to reduce by one-quarter. Add the demi-glace and reduce again by one-quarter. Pluck and finely chop the parsley leaves. Stir in the butter with a spoon. Strain the sauce, add the marrow and chopped parsley, and serve.

Morel sauce

This sauce is served with veal, but is also great with beef. The sauce is made while the meat is resting and in the same pan that the meat was fried in.

Makes 4 servings:
1 tablespoon butter
1 tablespoon finely chopped shallot
8 oz fresh morels
6 tablespoons port
6 tablespoons Veal Jus (See recipe page 26)
¼ cup crème fraîche
½ teaspoon salt
½ teaspoon pepper

Preparation:
Panfry the meat and set aside to rest. Add the butter in the pan over medium-high heat along with shallot and whole morels. There will be *suc*, or meat drippings, in the pan that will loosen when the butter, shallot, and morels are added. Let sizzle until the shallot and morels are lightly browned.

Deglaze the pan with port: Pour in a little of the port so that it fizzes in the pan. The liquid will help the *suc* loosen from the pan. When the fizzing stops, add the remaining port. Simmer and reduce the liquid by half.

Add the veal jus and crème fraîche. Simmer for an additional 5 minutes. Season with the salt and pepper and serve.

Goose liver sauce

Goose liver sauce is delicious served with sautéed foie gras (goose liver), goose liver ravioli, grilled chicken, or turkey.

Makes 4 servings:
6½ oz goose liver
½ teaspoon salt
½ teaspoon pepper
3 tablespoons Madeira
3 tablespoons cognac
6 tablespoons Chicken Jus
(See recipe page 19)
2 tablespoons crème fraîche
1 tablespoon butter

Preparation:
Cut the goose liver into large cubes. Reserve about one-third and sprinkle the rest well with the salt and pepper.

Place the seasoned goose liver in a smoking-hot deep sauté pan over high heat. Sauté until the pieces are well browned. Deglaze the pan with madeira. When you pour in the madeira, it will sizzle in the pan. Stir well, then simmer and reduce for 1–2 minutes. Pour in the cognac and immediately light it with a match. Let the flame extinguish on its own.

Stir in the chicken jus and crème fraîche, then pour the whole mixture into a pot. Place over the heat and blend the mixture with a hand-held mixer into a smooth sauce.

Mix the butter and the remaining goose liver in a separate bowl with the hand-held mixer. Stir the goose liver butter into the sauce with a spoon over low heat.

Strain the sauce and serve.

Steak and potatoes with pepper sauce

Makes 4 servings:

12 very small russet potatoes
2 tablespoons olive oil
1 clove garlic, peeled and crushed
½ teaspoon cracked black pepper
4 sirloin strip steaks, 6–7 oz each
Pepper Sauce (See recipe page 197)

Preparation:
Preheat the oven to 350°F. Wash and scrub the potatoes and cut lengthwise into wedges.

Heat the olive oil in a frying pan and brown the potatoes well. Transfer them to a roasting pan. Spread the garlic over the potatoes. Crack fresh pepper over the top. Bake the potatoes until tender when pierced, 20–30 minutes, depending on the size of the potatoes.

When the sauce and potatoes are ready, grill the meat over a hot flame, 3–5 minutes per side for rare to medium-rare. Serve the steaks accompanied with the sauce and the potatoes.

Marinades

A good marinade can improve the consistency of meat, elevate the flavor of a dish, and create an exciting contrast in flavors.

Yogurt marinade

Yogurt marinade is excellent for use with whole chickens and chicken breasts. It also gives lamb a Middle Eastern flair.

Makes 4 servings:

2 cups plain yogurt
2 crushed garlic cloves
3 tablespoons ground paprika
3 tablespoons curry powder
3 tablespoons ground ginger
½ teaspoon cayenne pepper
1 teaspoon salt

Preparation:
Mix the yogurt with the garlic, spices, and salt. Spread the marinade over the desired meat and refrigerate for at least 8 hours.

1. Mix the yogurt and all the seasonings, and the marinade is ready to use.

Lemon marinade

This marinade is great for chicken, turkey, veal, and even lamb. And, as you might expect, a lemon marinade is also excellent with fish, particularly sardines and shellfish, and with grilled vegetables.

Makes 4 servings:

Juice and zest of 2 lemons
6 tablespoons olive oil
1 teaspoon salt

Preparation:
Wash the lemons well. Grate the zest. Squeeze all the lemon juice into a bowl and mix with olive oil. Add the zest and salt.

Fish should marinate for just 1 hour. Marinated sardines will be ready to serve as is, while other fish must be cooked before serving.

White meat like chicken, veal, or pork should be marinated for 3 hours before cooking.

1. Mix olive oil with lemon juice, lemon zest, and salt.
The marinade is ready to use.

Barbecue marinade

As its name implies, this marinade should be used for spare ribs.

Makes 4 servings:
2 finely chopped onions
¼ cup cola
¼ cup soy sauce
2 tablespoons ketchup
½ tablespoon chopped red chile
1 tablespoon honey

Preparation:
Mix all the ingredients and rub over pork spare ribs. Marinate for at least 4 hours in the refrigerator before cooking.

Herb marinade

This is an excellent marinade for lamb.

Makes 4 servings:
2 cloves garlic
3 tablespoons finely chopped rosemary
2 tablespoons finely chopped thyme
1 tablespoon finely chopped flat-leaf parsley
1 finely chopped chile with seeds
1 tablespoon whole-grain mustard
1 teaspoon sugar
1 teaspoon salt
8 tablespoons olive oil

Preparation:
Peel and crush the garlic in a mortar to make a paste. Add the herbs and chile and mix well. Stir in mustard, sugar, and salt and blend in the oil at the end.

Meat should be marinated in the refrigerator for at least 8 hours.

Soy marinade

Use soy marinade with thin strips of beef that will be grilled. This marinade is used frequently in the Korean kitchen.

Makes 4 servings:
6 tablespoons soy sauce
2 cloves crushed garlic
1 tablespoon sugar
1 tablespoon sesame oil
1 tablespoon chopped green onion

Preparation:
Mix all the ingredients together. Meat should be marinated in the refrigerator for at least 8 hours.

Garlic marinade

Garlic marinade is delicious with lamb.

Makes 4 servings:
4 cloves garlic
¼ cup olive oil
1 tablespoon chopped fresh thyme
1 tablespoon chopped fresh rosemary
½ teaspoon salt

Preparation:
Peel and crush the garlic, then mix together with the other ingredients. Rub the marinade over meat and refrigerate for at least 6 hours.

Dessert sauces

These sauces shouldn't steal all the attention, but rather spotlight a dessert's main ingredient. Always be generous with the portions.

Chocolate sauce

This is a versatile all-around sauce, perfect for vanilla ice cream, milkshakes, poached pears, banana splits and anything else you want topped with a good chocolate sauce.

Makes 4 servings:

1¾ cups milk
6 tablespoons heavy cream
1 cup cocoa powder
3 oz bittersweet chocolate

Preparation:
Combine milk and cream in a saucepan and bring to a boil over medium heat. Remove from the heat and add the cocoa powder. Whisk well. Break the chocolate into small pieces and add to the pan. Whisk well until the chocolate has melted.

Pour the sauce through a sieve. Let cool (it will thicken as it cools) and serve.

1. Pour milk and heavy cream into a pan.

2. Bring to a boil and remove the pan from the heat. Add the cocoa powder.

3. Add the chocolate pieces and whisk well.

4. Strain the sauce, let cool, and serve.

Caramel sauce

Caramel sauce is a fine accompaniment to ice cream, poached fruit, and assorted tarts. For a real showstopper of a dessert, try it with a warm apple crumble with heavy cream.

Makes 4 servings:

4 tablespoons sugar
2 tablespoons water
¾ cup heavy cream

Preparation:
Mix sugar and water in a saucepan and heat over medium heat without stirring until the sugar has melted. (The water can be eliminated and, if so, the process will be expedited. If you choose to eliminate the water, pay very close attention.) As soon as the sugar is brown, take the pan off the heat.

Heat the heavy cream in a clean pan over medium-high heat. Just before it boils, remove from the heat and pour the warm cream over the browned sugar. Put the sugar mixture back on the heat and warm it up, stirring constantly. (Since the sugar can withstand a higher temperature than the cream, the sugar will stiffen when the cream is added. It is important to stir the entire time while the mixture is simmering, until the sugar and cream have mixed well.) The caramel sauce will gain a nice golden color little by little. As long as the sauce is warm, it will be thin. When it cools, it will thicken. It is not necessary to stir the sauce as it cools.

1. Mix the sugar and water in a pan.

2. Heat until the mixture is a golden color.

3. Whisk in the cream.

4. Let the sauce thicken as it cools, then serve.

Sangria sauce

This sauce is excellent served with poached fruit and vanilla ice cream.

Makes 4 servings:
2 cups red wine
1 vanilla pod
2 figs
8 strawberries
Zest and juice of 1 lemon
Zest and juice of 1 orange
⅓ cup sugar
1 cinnamon stick

Preparation:
Pour the red wine into a saucepan. Cut the vanilla pod in half lengthwise and scrape the seeds into the pan. Cut the figs in half. Hull the strawberries and cut in half. Add the fruit to the pan together with the remaining ingredients. Bring to a boil over medium heat.

Stir occasionally and simmer until the liquid has reduced to one-quarter of the original amount.

Strain the sauce and serve.

Vanilla sauce

This velvety vanilla sauce is delicious with everything from ice cream and chocolate pudding to filled puff pastries and apple tarts.

Makes 4 servings:
1 cup heavy cream
1 cup milk
1 vanilla pod
3 egg yolks
⅓ cup sugar

Preparation:
Combine the cream and milk in a saucepan over medium heat. Cut the vanilla pod in half lengthwise and scrape out the seeds. Add the pod and seeds to the pan. Bring to a boil, then set the pan aside.

Whisk together the egg yolks and sugar in a separate bowl.

Whisking vigorously, pour the warm milk mixture over the eggs. Pour the mixture back into the pan and place over medium heat. Stir continuously and carefully with a wooden spoon while the mixture heats up. The sauce should thicken, but never boil, or it will break and be ruined.

Strain through a fine sieve and let the sauce cool. It will continue to thicken as it cools. Serve.

Coffee sauce

Coffee sauce is delicious with vanilla ice cream, but perhaps best with a chocolate tart.

Makes 4 servings:
1 cup heavy cream
1 cup milk
3 tablespoons espresso
2 tablespoons coffee beans
3 egg yolks
⅓ cup sugar

Preparation:
Combine the cream, milk, espresso, and coffee beans in a saucepan. Bring to a boil and set aside.

Whisk together the egg yolks and sugar in a separate bowl.

Whisking vigorously, pour the warm milk and coffee mixture over the eggs. Pour the mixture back into the pan and place over medium heat. Stir continuously and carefully with a wooden spoon while the mixture heats up. The sauce should thicken, but never boil, or it will break and be ruined.

Strain through a fine sieve and let the sauce cool. It will continue to thicken as it cools. Serve.

Cilantro sauce

This sauce tastes fantastic on carpaccio of fruit, such as thin slices of pineapple or mango. It is also good served as a dip with melon kebabs.

Makes 4 servings:
6 tablespoons sugar
6 tablespoons water
1 teaspoon finely chopped fresh ginger
1 bunch fresh cilantro

Preparation:
Combine the sugar, water, and ginger in a pan over medium heat. Bring the mixture to a boil. Remove the pan from the heat and mix well.

Pluck the leaves from the cilantro and add them to the sugar syrup when it is cool.

Blend the mixture with a hand-held mixer and serve.

Mint sauce

This fresh and sweet sauce can be used as a dressing for strawberries or peach salad, as well as for fruit cocktail.

Makes 4 servings:
6 tablespoons sugar
6 tablespoons water
2 star anise pods
5 cardamom seeds
1 cinnamon stick
1 bunch fresh mint

Preparation:
Combine the sugar, water, star anise, cardamom seeds, and cinnamon stick in a pan over medium-high heat. Bring the mixture to a boil. Remove the pan from the heat and mix well.

Strain the sauce and let cool. Pluck the leaves from the mint and add them to the sugar syrup when it is cool. Serve.

Raspberry sauce

Raspberry sauce is a fantastic accompaniment to vanilla panna cotta, ice cream, or cheesecake.

Makes 4 servings:
1½ cups raspberries
2 tablespoons sugar
¼ cup water

Preparation:
Combine the raspberries, sugar, and water in a pan over medium heat. Cover and simmer for 15 minutes.

Strain the sauce, pressing with a spoon so that as much fruit flesh passes through the sieve as possible. This will remove the raspberry seeds. Serve.

This sauce can also be prepared without heat. Blend all the ingredients together with a hand-held mixer and pass the mixture through a sieve. This is called raspberry coulis.

Black currant sauce

Black currant sauce goes well with vanilla ice cream. Try it in a milkshake.

Makes 4 servings:
1½ cups fresh black currants
2 tablespoons sugar
¼ cup water

Preparation:
Combine the black currants, sugar, and water in a saucepan over medium heat. Cover and simmer for 15 minutes.

Strain the sauce, pressing with a spoon so that as much fruit flesh passes through the sieve as possible. Serve.

This sauce can also be prepared without heat. Blend all the ingredients together with a hand-held mixer and pass the mixture through a sieve. This is called black currant coulis.

Strawberry sauce

Strawberry sauce may be served with fruit tarts, fruit salad, strawberry cream cake, and crepes.

Makes 4 servings:
12 strawberries
2 tablespoons sugar
¼ cup water

Preparation:
Hull the strawberries and put them in a saucepan with the sugar and water. Cover and simmer over medium heat for 15 minutes.

Strain the sauce, pressing with a spoon so that as much fruit flesh passes through the sieve as possible. Serve.

This sauce can also be prepared without heat. Blend all the ingredients together with a hand-held mixer and pass the mixture through a sieve. This is called strawberry coulis.

Blueberry sauce

Try blueberry sauce on vanilla pudding or along-side blueberry pie.

Makes 4 servings:
1½ cups blueberries
2 tablespoons sugar
¼ cup water

Preparation:
Combine the blueberries, sugar, and water in a saucepan over medium heat. Cover and simmer for 15 minutes.

Blend the mixture with a hand-held mixer until smooth and serve.

This sauce can also be prepared without heat. Blend all the ingredients together with a hand-held mixer and pass the mixture through a sieve. This is called blueberry coulis.

Apricot sauce

Dolloped onto fresh summer fruit, this apricot sauce is unbelievably good.

Makes 4 servings:
12 fresh apricots
2 tablespoons sugar
¼ cup water

Preparation:
Halve and pit the apricots. Combine the apricots, sugar, and water in a saucepan over medium heat. Cover and simmer for 15 minutes.

Blend the mixture with a hand-held mixer until smooth and serve.

This sauce can also be prepared without heat. Blend all the ingredients together with a hand-held mixer and pass the mixture through a sieve. This is called apricot coulis.

Peach sauce

Peach sauce is a perfect accompaniment to poached peaches and vanilla ice cream, but can also be used to sprinkle over the base of a layer cake, especially a strawberry whipped-cream cake.

Makes 4 servings:
3 fresh peaches
2 tablespoons sugar
¼ cup water

Preparation:
Peel the peaches, halve and remove the pits, and cut the flesh into wedges. Combine the wedges in a saucepan with the sugar and water. Place a lid over the top and simmer for 15 minutes over medium heat.

Blend the mixture with a hand-held mixer until smooth and serve.

This sauce can also be prepared without heat. Blend all the ingredients together with a hand-held mixer, and pass the mixture through a sieve. This is called peach coulis.

Apple sauce

Apple sauce is divine with cinnamon ice cream or apple cake. The sauce can be served with plain yogurt as a healthy and simple dessert.

Makes 4 servings:
2 apples
2 tablespoons sugar
3 tablespoons water
1 cinnamon stick
1 vanilla pod

Preparation:
Peel and core the apples and cut them into wedges. Combine the wedges in a saucepan together with the sugar, water, and cinnamon stick. Cut the vanilla pod in half lengthwise, scrape out the seeds, and add the pod and seeds to the pan. Let the mixture simmer over medium heat, covered, for 30 minutes.

Remove the cinnamon stick and vanilla pod. Blend the mixture with a hand-held mixer until smooth and serve.

Pineapple sauce

Pineapple sauce complements grilled pineapple, while the pineapple coulis works especially well with fresh sorbets.

Makes 4 servings:
½ pineapple
2 tablespoons sugar
3 tablespoons water

Preparation:
Peel the pineapple and cut it into chunks. Combine with the sugar and water in a saucepan over medium heat. Cover and simmer for 15 minutes.

Blend the mixture with a hand-held mixer until smooth and serve.

This sauce can also be prepared without heat. Blend all the ingredients together with a hand-held mixer and pass the mixture through a sieve. This is called pineapple coulis.

Fruit salad with strawberry sauce

Make 4 servings:

½ pineapple
2 oranges
1 bunch grapes
2 bananas
8 slices watermelon
Juice of 1 lime
Strawberry Sauce (See recipe page 231)
Chiffonade of fresh mint

Preparation:
Peel the pineapple, cut it into rounds, and cut out the tough core. Cut the pineapple flesh into strips. Peel the oranges and cut out the sections of flesh between the membranes. Wash the grapes, leaving them as a bunch. Peel the bananas and slice them on the diagonal. Cut the watermelon into slices and remove the rind.

Arrange the fruit on serving plates. Drizzle with the lime juice and strawberry sauce, and sprinkle the finely sliced mint over the top.

Matching dishes with sauces

APPLE CAKE
- Apple Sauce for dessert

APPLE CRISP OR COBBLER
- Caramel Sauce

ASPARAGUS
- Hollandaise
- Morel Cream
- Mousseline

AVOCADO
- Cocktail Sauce

BACON, crisp
- Pepper Sauce

BANANA SPLIT
- Chocolate Sauce

BEEF
- Aioli
- Beef Jus
- Béarnaise
- Beurre Maître d'Hôtel
- Bordelaise
- Cambridge Sauce
- Cauliflower Sauce
- Choron Sauce
- Cognac Sauce
- Fig Sauce
- Garlic Butter
- Herb Butter
- Horseradish Cream
- Horseradish Dip
- Madeira Sauce
- Morel Sauce
- Pepper Sauce
- Ravigotte Sauce
- Rémoulade
- Roquefort Cream
- Sauce Chateaubriand
- Sauce Diablo
- Soy Marinade
- Tarragon Sauce
- Tartar Sauce
- Tomato Salsa
- Tomato Sauce

BLUEBERRY PIE
- Blueberry Sauce

CHEESECAKE
- Raspberry Sauce

CHÈVRE
- Honey Vinaigrette
- Tapenade Vinaigrette

CHICKEN, grilled, roasted, sautéed, or stewed
- Apple Sauce for meat
- Chicken Jus
- Duck Jus
- Eggplant Salsa
- Goose Liver Sauce
- Lemon Marinade
- Madeira Sauce
- Mushroom Cream
- Mustard Cream
- Parmesan Mayonnaise
- Pepper Sauce
- Pheasant Jus
- Port Wine Sauce
- Sauce Périgueux
- Squab Jus
- Tomato Salsa
- Veal Jus
- Yogurt Dip
- Yogurt Marinade

CHOCOLATE PUDDING
- Vanilla Sauce

EGG, hard-boiled
- Aioli
- Avocado Dip
- Flat-Leaf Parsley Vinaigrette
- Mayonnaise
- Mornay Sauce

FISH, grilled, sautéed, or poached
- Aioli
- Anchoïade
- Anchovy Butter
- Asparagus Sauce
- Béarnaise
- Beef Jus
- Beurre Blanc
- Beurre Maître d'Hôtel
- Beurre Meunière
- Beurre Noisette
- Cambridge Sauce
- Carrot Jus
- Caulifower Sauce
- Champagne Sauce
- Choron Sauce
- Fish Velouté
- Garlic Butter
- Garlic Dip
- Grenobloise Butter
- Herb Butter
- Herb Dip
- Horseradish Cream
- Lemon Marinade
- Mayonnaise

- Morel Cream
- Pea Sauce
- Pepper Salsa
- Pesto
- Ravigotte Sauce
- Red Beet Sauce
- Rémoulade
- Salsa Verde
- Sauce Albert
- Squash Salsa
- Tarragon Sauce
- Tartar Sauce
- Tomato Salsa
- Tomato Sauce

FISH CASSEROLE
- Fish Velouté
- Mussel Stock
- Vegetable Stock

FISH SOUP
- Mussel Stock
- Rouille

FRUIT
- Apricot Sauce for dessert

FRUIT CARPACCIO
- Cilantro Sauce

FRUIT COCKTAIL
- Mint Sauce

FRUIT, grilled or poached
- Caramel Sauce
- Chocolate Sauce
- Peach Sauce
- Sangria Sauce
- Strawberry Sauce

FRUIT, sautéed
- Port Wine Sauce

GELATIN
- Vanilla Sauce

GNOCCHI
- Rabbit Jus

GRUYÈRE
- Rouille

ICE CREAM
- Apple Sauce
- Black Currant Sauce
- Caramel Sauce
- Chocolate Sauce
- Coffee Sauce

- Raspberry Sauce
- Sangria Sauce
- Strawberry Sauce
- Vanilla Sauce

LAMB, grilled, sautéed, or stewed
- Apricot Sauce for meat
- Cognac Sauce
- Eggplant Salsa
- Garlic Marinade
- Herb Cream
- Herb Marinade
- Lamb Jus
- Lemon Marinade
- Sauce Diablo
- Squash Salsa
- Tarragon Sauce
- Tomato Salsa
- Yogurt Marinade

LENTILS
- Red Beet Sauce
- Tomato Sauce

LIVER, sautéed chicken, duck, and goose liver
- Fig Sauce
- Goose Liver Sauce
- Grape Sauce
- Port Wine Sauce

LOBSTER, baked, boiled, or sautéed
- Avocado Dip
- Champagne Sauce
- Cocktail Sauce
- Lobster Jus
- Shellfish Jus

MELON
- Cilantro Sauce

MILKSHAKE
- Black Currant Sauce
- Chocolate Sauce

OCTOPUS, grilled
- Chile Vinaigrette

OYSTERS
- Shallot Vinaigrette

PANCAKES
- Strawberry Sauce

PASTA
- Asparagus Sauce

- Carrot Jus
- Lobster Jus
- Mushroom Cream
- Pea Sauce
- Pesto
- Tomato Sauce

PASTA GRATINEE
- Béchamel

PEACH SALAD
- Mint Sauce

PINEAPPLE, grilled
- Pineapple Sauce

PIZZA
- Olive Salsa
- Pesto

POMMES FRITES
- Aioli
- Béarnaise
- Mayonnaise

PORK
- Apple Sauce for meat
- Cognac Sauce
- Mustard Cream
- Pork Jus
- Prune Sauce
- Sauce Diablo
- White Onion Sauce

POT-AU-FEU
- Herb Butter

POTATO, baked, boiled, or fried
- Garlic Butter
- Garlic Dip
- Horseradish Cream
- Horseradish Dip
- White Onion Sauce

POTATO CHIPS
- Garlic Dip
- Roquefort Dip

POULTRY
- Cognac Sauce
- Duck Jus
- Pheasant Jus
- Pigeon Jus
- Port Wine Sauce
- Prune Sauce
- Sauce Diablo
- Sauce Périgueux

PUFF PASTRY
- Vanilla Sauce

RABBIT
- Rabbit Jus

RICE
- Asparagus Sauce
- Tomato Sauce

SALAD
- Aioli
- Balsamic Vinaigrette
- Caesar Dressing
- Cocktail Sauce
- Flat-Leaf Parsley Vinaigrette
- Garlic Mayonnaise
- Honey Vinaigrette
- Lemon Vinaigrette
- Mustard Vinaigrette
- Olive Salsa
- Parmesan Mayonnaise
- Pesto
- Shallot Vinaigrette
- Tapenade Vinaigrette
- Tomato Salsa
- Yogurt Dip

SANDWICHES
- Mayonnaise

SCALLOPS
- Beef Jus

SHELLFISH
- Avocado Dip
- Beurre Blanc
- Cocktail Sauce
- Lemon marinade
- Lemon Vinaigrette
- Lobster Jus
- Ravigotte Sauce
- Sauce Albert
- Shellfish Jus
- Tartar Sauce

SHELLFISH SALAD
- Chile Vinaigrette
- Cocktail Sauce
- Shallot Vinaigrette

SHELLFISH SOUP
- Rouille

SNAILS
- Aioli

SPARE RIBS
- Barbecue Marinade

STRAWBERRY SALAD
- Mint Sauce

STRAWBERRY WHIPPED CREAM CAKE
- Peach Sauce
- Strawberry Sauce

TARTS
- Caramel Sauce
- Coffee Sauce
- Strawberry Sauce
- Vanilla Sauce

TOAST
- Anchovy Butter
- Avocado Dip
- Eggplant Salsa
- Olive Salsa
- Pepper Salsa
- Roquefort Dip
- Rouille

TOMATO AND MOZZARELLA
- Basil Vinaigrette

TOMATO SALAD
- Squash Salsa

TORTILLA CHIPS
- Avocado Dip
- Tomato Salsa

TURKEY
- Goose Liver Sauce
- Lemon Marinade

VANILLA PANNA COTTA
- Raspberry Sauce

VANILLA PUDDING
- Blueberry Sauce

VEAL
- Apple Sauce for meat
- Cognac Sauce
- Fig Sauce
- Lemon Marinade
- Madeira Sauce
- Morel Cream
- Prune Sauce
- Roquefort Cream
- Sauce Chateaubriand

- Tartar Sauce
- Tomato Salsa
- Veal Jus

VEGETABLES, raw
- Aioli
- Anchoyade
- Avocado Dip
- Béarnaise
- Cambridge Sauce
- Garlic Dip
- Garlic Mayonnaise
- Herb Dip
- Horseradish Cream
- Horseradish Dip
- Pea Sauce
- Roquefort Dip
- Tartar Sauce
- Yogurt Dip

VEGETABLES, gratinée
- Béchamel
- Mornay Sauce

WILD FOWL
- Bordelaise
- Fig Sauce
- Sauce Chasseur

WILD GAME
- Bordelaise
- Cumberland Sauce
- Sauce Chasseur

Alphabetical recipe index

SAUCE
Photographer **Morten Brun**
Designer **Therese Jacobsen**
Translator (English edition) **Scott Givot**
Proofreader (English edition) **Kate Washington**

Thanks to **Laurent Surville**

Set in FS Albert
Printed and bound in Singapore by **Tien Wah Press**
First printed in 2008.
10 9 8 7 6 5 4 3 2 1

ISBN-13: 978-1-934533-14-7
ISBN-10: 1-934533-14-9

WELDON OWEN INC.
Chief Executive Officer, Weldon Owen Group **John Owen**
President and Chief Executive Officer, Weldon Owen Inc. **Terry Newell**
Director of Finance **Mark Perrigo**
VP, International Sales **Stuart Laurence**
VP, Sales & New Business Development **Amy Kaneko**
VP & Creative Director **Gaye Allen**
VP & Publisher **Hannah Rahill**
Associate Publisher **Amy Marr**
Executive Editor **Sarah Putman Clegg**
Production Designer **Meghan Hildebrand**
Production Director **Chris Hemesath**
Production Manager **Michelle Duggan**
Color Manager **Teri Bell**

Original title: SAUS
Copyright © VERSAL FORLAG, Oslo 2007
English translation © 2008 by Weldon Owen Inc.

Library of Congress Cataloging-in-Publication data is available.

Weldon Owen Inc.
415 Jackson Street, San Francisco, CA 94111
Telephone: 415 291 0100 Fax: 415 291 8841
www.weldonowen.com

Note: Some of the recipes in this book call for
uncooked or semicooked eggs, which carry a slight
risk of salmonella. This risk is of most concern to small
children, the elderly, pregnant women, and anyone
with a compromised immune system. Use your best
judgment in serving or enjoying such recipes.

An imprint of Weldon Owen Inc.